M000236500

THELEMA

Julie Rancourt Photography

About the Author

Colin Campbell (New Hampshire) has been studying and teaching elements of magical practice for over twenty-five years with a particular emphasis on Thelema, giving lectures at both the local and national level. He is the author of several books, including *A Concordance to the Holy Books of Thelema* (2008), *The Magic Seal of Dr. John Dee: The Sigillum Dei Aemeth* (2009), *The Offices of Spirit* (2011), and *Of the Arte Goetia* (2015).

To Write to the Author

If you wish to contact the author or would like more information about this book, please write to the author in care of Llewellyn Worldwide, and we will forward your request. Both the author and publisher appreciate hearing from you and learning of your enjoyment of this book and how it has helped you. Llewellyn Worldwide cannot guarantee that every letter written to the author can be answered, but all will be forwarded. Please write to:

Colin Campbell
℅ Llewellyn Worldwide
2143 Wooddale Drive
Woodbury, MN 55125-2989

Please enclose a self-addressed stamped envelope for reply,
or $1.00 to cover costs. If outside the USA, enclose
an international postal reply coupon.

COLIN D. CAMPBELL

THELEMA

———

An Introduction to the Life, Work & Philosophy of
ALEISTER CROWLEY

Foreword by Lon Milo DuQuette

Llewellyn Worldwide
Woodbury, Minnesota

Thelema: An Introduction to the Life, Work & Philosophy of Aleister Crowley © 2018 by Colin D. Campbell. All rights reserved. No part of this book may be used or reproduced in any manner whatsoever, including internet usage, without written permission from Llewellyn Publications, except in the case of brief quotations embodied in critical articles and reviews.

FIRST EDITION
First Printing, 2018

Book design by Bob Gaul
Cover design by Kevin R. Brown
Interior illustrations by Llewellyn art department except on pages 125–130 by Wen Hsu
Interior photos courtesy of the Ordo Templi Orientis (O.T.O.)

Llewellyn Publications is a registered trademark of Llewellyn Worldwide Ltd.

Library of Congress Cataloging-in-Publication Data (Pending)
ISBN: 978-0-7387-5104-7

Llewellyn Worldwide Ltd. does not participate in, endorse, or have any authority or responsibility concerning private business transactions between our authors and the public.

All mail addressed to the author is forwarded, but the publisher cannot, unless specifically instructed by the author, give out an address or phone number.

Any internet references contained in this work are current at publication time, but the publisher cannot guarantee that a specific location will continue to be maintained. Please refer to the publisher's website for links to authors' websites and other sources.

Llewellyn Publications
A Division of Llewellyn Worldwide Ltd.
2143 Wooddale Drive
Woodbury, MN 55125-2989
www.llewellyn.com

Printed in the United States of America

I dedicate this book to Aleister Crowley and to all Thelemites who were, and are, and are to come.

Acknowledgments

I would like to thank Ordo Templi Orientis for allowing me to use the copious references to Crowley's work (and images) that were necessary to adequately explain his life, philosophy, and practices, all of which are in their careful custody. We owe them a debt of gratitude in the protection and preservation of the legacy of the Master Therion.

I would like to express my sincere appreciation to Henrik Bogdan and Katherine Palakovich. I would also like to thank Cheri Gaudet, Michael Estell, and James Strain for their thoughtful review and comments on the work in progress, as well as Lon Milo DuQuette for his kind foreword.

Contents

Foreword

Then saith the prophet and slave of the beauteous one: Who am I, and what shall be the sign? So she answered him, bending down, a lambent flame of blue, all-touching, all penetrant, her lovely hands upon the black earth, & her lithe body arched for love, and her soft feet not hurting the little flowers: Thou knowest! And the sign shall be my ecstasy, the consciousness of the continuity of existence, the omnipresence of my body.

—*Liber AL vel Legis,* I. V. 26.

Do what thou wilt shall be the whole of the Law.

Aleister Crowley died in 1947 at the age of seventy-two. The whereabouts of his ashes remain a mystery. For twenty years after his death, his name and his voluminous writings remained for the most part undiscovered, unread, and unappreciated by all but a tiny band of former disciples, bohemian artists, and a handful of revolutionary thinkers. Then, on June 1, 1967, Crowley's unmistakable visage appeared (glaring out at us from between the faces of Indian holy man Swami Sri Yukteswar and sex goddess Mae West) on the (then) most eagerly awaited *objet d'art* on the planet—the album cover of the Beatles' newest LP, *Sgt. Pepper's Lonely Hearts Club Band.*

The cover art was the creation of artist Peter Blake, who wanted to surround the band with what he called "a magical crowd." The inclusion of Swami Sri Yukteswar, Paramahansa Yogananda, and other Hindu yogis was George Harrison's idea. Among characters John Lennon "liked" was the poet and "wickedest man in the world" Aleister Crowley.

Do not misunderstand me. I'm not suggesting that the Beatles or Peter Blake were directly responsible for the spiritual and cultural upheavals of the 1960s or the storms that are still echoing (actively or reactively) in today's chaotic world. Nor am I suggesting John Lennon or Peter Blake should be singled out and credited for igniting the revival of interest and appreciation of Aleister Crowley, Thelema, magick, or any of the progressive spiritual movements that continue to proliferate today. Like all great artists at pivotal moments in history, these sensitive pioneers were merely among the first to react and respond to the effects of a dramatic shift in human consciousness.

Consciously or subconsciously, their works gave voice to the new reality. The art they and their contemporaries created during those golden years pealed like a mighty bell that vibrated with the master "note" of this new universal consciousnes, a note that rang out like a broadcast signal that triggered sympathetic responses in the hearts and souls of all who were poised and ripe for awakening.

The concept of evolving shifts in consciousness is not a new one. Almost every ancient culture had its version of "ages" (i.e., the Golden Age, when humanity *walked with the gods*, or the Dark Age, when the gods abandoned us). The Hindus call the various ages *Yugas*, [1] which predictively rise and fall in cycles of thousands of millennia as our entire solar system careens around the galactic center in a huge elliptical orbit.

---

[1]   I can't resist pointing out an amazing coincidence. One of the most respected Hindu experts on Yugas was Swami Sri Yukteswar, the man standing beside Aleister Crowley on the cover of *Sgt. Pepper's Lonely Hearts Club Band*.

Astrologers have their own version of the cosmic cycles based on the apparent backward movement of the signs of the zodiac relative to the position of the rising sun on the spring equinox. It takes 2,160 years to traverse one complete sign, and most astrologers compute that we have recently passed (or will soon pass) from the astrological Age of Pisces into the Age of Aquarius.

Now, you may think it odd that I should begin these introductory words to Mr. Campbell's marvelous book about Thelema by talking about 1960s pop stars and Hindu theories of astrology, but (in *my* mind, at least) it illustrates the most important thing to first understand when attempting to comprehend the meaning and significance of Thelema; that is, whether any of us are consciously aware of it or not, within the last hundred years or so there has been a profound and dramatic shift (advance, transformation, mutation, amendment, metamorphosis, transfiguration, leap, refocus) in human consciousness. We are all now functioning in an entirely new and different reality than the one in which our recent ancestors functioned. The old ways of doing business on every level of our lives will never again work exactly like they used to.

It's not just the fact that our tastes have changed or that we hear music or appreciate art differently; it's not just the fact that our understanding of mathematics has exploded *inwardly* to irrational quantum levels or that our understanding of astronomy has exploded *outwardly* and erased all old time and dimensional limitations; it's not just the fact that many of the most fortunate among us have the store of ten thousand years of human knowledge at our electronic fingertips or that many of us are now routinely accustomed to educational, social, and economic liberties. No. All these things are simply symptoms and by-products of a new essential factor in the great formula of human consciousness. The new factor isn't anything complex or particularly esoteric. It is, however, significant enough to cause a new mutation in the DNA of our consciousness. The new factor is simply this: *A new level of self-awareness.*

This might not sound very sexy or dramatic, but, in this *new* reality, *nothing* could be *more* sexy or dramatic. This new awakening is disarmingly simple and fundamental. But, like the invisible wind, its existence only makes itself known by the effects it has on other things. It's really hard to make observations about self-awareness because the observer is the object being observed. Actually, the whole thing is simpler than it sounds. Allow me to offer an illustration of shifts in self-awareness.

Our very ancient ancestors, while being cognizant of day and night, darkness and light, heat and cold, comfort and discomfort, were primarily focused on day-to-day, moment-to-moment issues of immediate self-preservation. All human activities, whether conscious or instinctual, revolved around the preservation of the body through protection, nourishment, and the biological perpetuation of the species. All other observations or speculations about life or the world around us were projected against the screen of this reality and interpreted to satisfy these immediate needs. Everything about our ancestors' conscious and subconscious lives (religious concepts and expressions, gods, spirits, myths, rituals, even art) was interpreted by the self-identity of a creature competing with other creatures for food and survival.

The metaphoric "Gods" that visibly ruled this level of consciousness-reality were the earth itself and the earth's human equivalent, woman, in particular the Mother. Crowley named this phase of evolutionary consciousness the Aeon of Isis after the great Egyptian Mother Goddess.

Eventually, as our understanding of the world around us increased a bit, our self-awareness shifted and received a fine-tuning. We started to see ourselves as existing in a more complex and wondrous environment that we could partially manage and control. No longer did we see ourselves only as just another competing creature but as a master creature that could exploit other creatures and our environment. If we were cold, we could build or even travel to warmer lands. If we were hungry, we could cultivate plants rather than forage for them. We could domesticate and breed beasts rather than hunt them. Our eyes turned to the sky and it became evident that the sun made the plants grow and lured animals to come eat the plants. Summer and winter were sun-triggered events that needed to be dealt with. Gods and religions evolved to accommodate the new reality—the new self-identity. Existence was now seen as a partnership of sun and earth, father and mother.

But along with this wakening came the new mystery formula—the formula of a sun that dies every day and almost dies every winter. And this new formula brought with it our terrible preoccupation with death. Plants die and the dead seeds are buried and then magically reborn; the sun dies and needs to be magically resurrected; it only follows that *I* die and *I* will need to be magically brought back to life.

Crowley named this phase of evolutionary consciousness the Aeon of Osiris after the great Egyptian god of death and resurrection. It is a formula based on our self-identity with the sun which dies and is magically reborn. It is the level of consciousness that has fashioned the reality of our most recent ancestors—their religion, politics, war, culture, art, literature, civilization itself: everything.

All that has changed. While the decaying zombie remnants of the Aeon of Osiris will likely haunt us for the foreseeable future, a new age has dawned. Crowley named this new phase of evolutionary consciousness the Aeon of Horus, the child of Isis and Osiris. Instead of our conscious reality arising from the need for nourishment (as in the Aeon of Isis), or our obsession with overcoming death (as in the Aeon of Osiris), we now simply grow as naturally, as innocently, and as joyously as a child—a child who will accept no limits to its potential growth.

As unbelievably simple as it sounds, the factor that characterizes the essence of our new self-identity, the factor that characterizes our new level of consciousness, is our universally accepted observation that the *sun does not die*. It shines eternally. This simple new reality has permanently upgraded the operating system of human consciousness. The sun does not die. We do not die. The sun shines eternally—we shine eternally. We now function as a unit of self-awareness that deep down inside knows it does not die, that knows there is no off switch, that knows we've always been *on* and we'll always be *on*.

In the Aeon of Horus, eternal life is now simply understood as "the consciousness of the continuity of existence."

Like Lao Tzu's mysterious Tao, Thelema defies objective definition.

Is it a philosophy? Although there are philosophical nuances to Thelema, it is bigger than philosophy. But, if we were to attempt to explain Thelema to someone who needs to approach things from a philosophic angle, we could say "Thelema is a rational philosophy of spiritual self-sufficiency."

Is it a religion? Although there are infinite ways to incorporate your understanding of Thelema in religious forms of expression, Thelema is bigger than religion. But, if we were to attempt to explain Thelema to someone that needs to approach things from a classic religious angle, we could say, "Thelema is a rational religion of sun worship ... if you define the word *sun* as also meaning yourself."

Is it a magical system? Although many magicians consider themselves Thelemites, Thelema is bigger than any particular system, technique, or study. Indeed, once one has comfortably adjusted to the new level of self-awareness, Thelema serves only to enhance, energize, and hybridize whatever philosophical, religious, or magical systems or schools of thought you hold dear.

Is it Crowley's magical societies, O.T.O. and A∴A∴? Although these two organizations propagate the Law of Thelema and the teachings of Aleister, Thelema is bigger that any organization, order, or school of instruction. As a matter of fact, Thelema is bigger than *The Book of the Law*, or Aleister Crowley, or anything in heaven or Earth ... but *you*.

—Love is the law, love under will.
Lon Milo DuQuette

Do what thou wilt shall be the whole of the Law.
                                    —Aleister Crowley

Introduction

Aleister Crowley was an enigmatic and complicated man by any standard, and would have been so had he never picked up the mantle of the magician. Given a lifetime of work by a prolific author—coupled with several lifetimes' worth of controversy!—it is no wonder that so many people miss the point of Crowley entirely. It is easier to simply shrug one's shoulders, accept the popular opinion, and accept his reputation as "the wickedest man in the world." That's the danger of a dialectic: you miss all the finer points that linger between the black and the white.

When I first encountered Crowley, though I had studied magick for several years, I wasn't sure what to make of him either. I could tell that he was a genius and that he was speaking at a level I did not fully understand. While many of the things he wrote shocked my sensibilities, I also had a growing suspicion that there was something more going on than what was presented on the page. There were points where he was deliberately provocative, brazenly and even absurdly savage, yet I could not help but feel that it was written in a way that was meant to conceal something deeper. I would also come to recognize that some of those same sensibilities Crowley was challenging, ideas that I considered fundamental to who I was as a person, were in fact holding me back from the person I was meant to be. Such, one may argue, is the nature of illumination.

One of the principal problems with Crowley is that you must read a lot of his work to even begin to understand what he is trying to convey. He can be exceptionally difficult for the beginner, writing as he did in veiled analogy and with reference to contemporary events that stymie even those well acquainted with the man and his work. At times it can feel like having half an equation, with the other half scattered across a dozen or so other unreferenced texts, if even there. Include the fact that he quite literally could not put certain ideas in print without trouble from the authorities, especially ideas related to sex, putting the pieces together can be difficult. All I can say is keep reading.

In writing *this* work, keeping a consistently narrow scope of introductory material was paramount. Those familiar with Crowley will argue, "Why didn't you include…!" for one thing or another, which is fair enough. Not only did I recognize that any manageable introduction to Crowley would be inadequate, *I have counted on it.* For this reason, additional references and suggestions for further reading are included within the chapters themselves. From here, those interested in Crowley can begin looking deeper into his written works with some sense of direction and a foundation of basic knowledge. It is my sincere wish that anyone reading this ultimately comes to a point where they understand enough to say how they would have done it better!

My approach is to address Crowley in three distinct phases: history, philosophy, and practice. I begin with a short biography, since to understand Crowley's life helps to better understand the context from which his philosophies arose. The second section begins to unfold that philosophy itself, Thelema, a word that means "will" in Greek. Finally, practices common to *Thelemites*, practitioners or followers of Thelema, are given to provide the reader an understanding of the practices identifiable with, if not unique to, Crowley's legacy.

Now, to the point: *Why Thelema?* What, says the hardened critic, could the obtuse mystical philosophies of an eccentric, Victorian-born, middling poet, sexual deviant, devil worshipper, and drug addict possibly have to offer me? Such obviously biased and salacious accusations aside, now, as then, the answer is simple: Crowley shows us a method for spiritual attainment that focuses on the uniqueness of the individual rather than conformance to a creed, and one that ultimately leads you to the understanding of your own innate divinity. Casting aside aeons of adherence to a social order dominated by the impossible gods of sacrifice and restriction, Thelema represents a new age of spiritual development that empowers us all to discover our True Self through the manifestation of our True Will.

"Success is thy proof: argue not, convert not, talk not overmuch!"
—*The Book of the Law*, Chapter III, Verse 42

Onion Peelings[2]

The Universe is the Practical Joke of the General at the Expense of the Particular, quoth Frater Perdurabo, and laughed.

But those disciples nearest to him wept, seeing the Universal Sorrow.

Those next to them laughed, seeing the Universal Joke.

Below these certain disciples wept.

Then certain laughed.

Others next wept.

Others next laughed.

Next others wept.

Next others laughed.

Last came those who wept because they could not see the Joke, and those that laughed lest they should be thought not to see the Joke, and thought it safe to act like Frater Perdurabo.

---

2 Crowley, "Ch. 14: Onion Peelings," *The Book of Lies*, 1995.

But though Frater Perdurabo laughed openly, He also at the same time wept secretly; and in himself he neither laughed nor wept.

Nor did he mean what he said.

Man, Myth,
and Legend

To write an even mildly passable biography of Aleister Crowley is a monumental task, and a measure I shall not attempt to meet within the scope of this work. Toward that end, Crowley left *The Confessions of Aleister Crowley*, his own *autohagiography*, the first sections of which were published in two volumes in 1929, with the full work being issued post-humously in 1969.[3] More recent times have seen exceptional research on his life by historians and scholars of Western esotericism that have resulted in several well-crafted biographies, to which reference will be given and the reader can inquire for greater detail.

My intentions are instead to present a brief sketch of Crowley's life, highlighting the events that will better explain the man and ultimately the philosophy behind Thelema, his spiritual legacy. From a life of privilege as the sole heir of his father's fortune, to his death in penury after having spent everything and then some in pursuit of his art, Crowley was—and

---

3   An *autohagiography* is the autobiography of a saint, a tongue-in-cheek wordplay of
the sort Crowley reveled in.

is—an enigmatic, complex, and controversial figure. Much of the *legend* that has become Crowley's legacy stems from sensational accounts fabricated to titillate the public—then, as now, eager for the first scent of scandal—but they also arise from many of his own writings. He reveled in his reputation, which he did little to discourage when writing in metaphors that would shock even a modern reader not already informed on the underlying meaning of his analogies.

While both vilified and celebrated in his own lifetime and beyond, one finds in Crowley an exceptional man, yet a man not without his flaws, as one might expect of anyone who dares greatly. Yet this was part of the draw for me: Crowley the man in all his flawed humanity, and Crowley who had also ascended to the heights (and depths) of spiritual attainment. It speaks to the fact that spiritual attainment is not a point-event, a single moment in time where we are forever-after an enlightened being. We must inevitably come crashing back to our earthly egos, though perhaps with a better command and control of it, and fight the many forces that might pervert its best intentions.

And it is with the best of intentions that we begin.

Birth and Early Childhood

By his own account, Aleister Crowley was born on October 12, 1875, to Edward and Emily (Bishop) Crowley at 30 Clarendon Square in Leamington in Warwickshire, England, at about eleven at night. His given name was Edward, after his father and his father's father, with a middle name of Alexander: hence, in full, Edward Alexander Crowley. As a boy, he went by a shortened form of his middle name, *Alick*, a household convenience to differentiate him from his father. It would still be some years before he donned the *nom de plume*—or is it *nom de guerre*?—of Aleister.

Situated somewhat evenly between London and Birmingham, the bustling town of Leamington Spa was renowned for its saline baths, the purported curative and restorative properties being responsible for the surge in popularity and affluence since its first bathhouse was opened to the public in 1786. At Clarendon Square, the Crowley home was one of the many fine Georgian-era townhouses erected in the necessity of the town's expansion, the population at that time being approximately 25,000—no small borough for what was not long before simply a "farm on the river Leam," from whence the town got its name. This bustling resort for England's elite was young Alick's home until he was five, at which point the family moved to Redhill, Surrey, a southern suburb of greater London.

Crowley's father was independently wealthy as a result of a very successful family brewing business in Alton, to the southwest of London. He had foregone this line of work, however, on the religious grounds of abstaining from alcohol, having taken up the faith of the evangelical Exclusive Plymouth Brethren. A sect begun most notably by John Nelson Darby in the early part of the nineteenth century in rejection of the predominant Anglican Church, the Plymouth Brethren believed not only that common people could take communion together, but that scripture was to be interpreted as the ultimate authority: above tradition and certainly above the political expediencies toward which the Anglican Church was inclined in its relationship with the British government.

Crowley notes with no small sense of admiration that his father, in true evangelical style, would often go about town and casually engage people on the topic of what they were planning to do that day, adding continually "...and then?" until such a point as they arrived at their inevitable death—which of course would prompt the same question: "And then?" There was never a more successful tool of promulgation than the fear of eternal hellfire, a fear that likely bore a heavier weight on the promulgator than his intended convert. Crowley is likely to have taken much from this memory of his father in developing his own spiritual philosophy, far removed as it may have been from the austerity of that religious sect. He commonly declared to friends and strangers alike, "Do what thou wilt shall be the whole of the Law!" upon first greeting.

Despite the Plymouth Brethren being exceedingly close-knit, forbidding even association with individuals external to their religious group, Aleister was afforded all the luxuries of his social class, including private tutors and boarding schools throughout his early education. Given the strong religious leanings of his family, these were also staunchly evangelical, teaching all but exclusively from the Bible. Crowley claims no small happiness in this period, despite being at odds with the man we would come to know. Why would he not? Since he viewed his father as the "wealthy scion of a race of Quakers," it seemed logical that he would be heir to no less a claim. Yet it was precisely at this point, on the brink of manhood and with all the world before him, that his life fell apart.

Crowley was just eleven when his father was diagnosed with cancer of the tongue. [4] The family ultimately decided on a treatment approach that is now understood as nothing more than medical quackery in lieu of the standard medical practice of the time, limited as it was. The decision ultimately proved fatal, something that Crowley never quite forgave. The death of his father in March of 1887 left him to the care of his mother and her family, an arrangement that he came to despise. While Crowley idealized his father as a kind and rational man of religion, he saw his mother as little more than an unthinking zealot, having been converted to the faith of his father rather than having arrived at it of her own accord. Where the father saw context and adjustment, the mother saw only rules that were to be followed. Darker days were to come.

The family inherited his father's wealth, and Crowley continued to be educated at private religious boarding schools, but seemingly one worse than the next in its fervor for discipline—a penchant for cruelty well-known in private schools at the time and exacerbated by the stern environment of religious extremism in which he was entrenched. Coupled

---

4   It is tempting to consider that Edward Sr. might have contracted cancer from smoking, the dangers of which were certainly less known at the time, but Crowley notes in *Confessions* (p. 71) that his father never suffered such a vice.

with Crowley's emotional lashing-out in the wake of his father's death, it combined for many years of misery at what can readily be described as the hands of sociopathic sadists armed with the unrelenting authority of a self-righteous religious fervor. It was a misery that he would not soon forget, and equally served to forge the man that came to call himself by a name his frustrated mother bestowed upon him: *The Beast*.

Early Adulthood

It was a difficult time for Crowley. The death of his father robbed him of his assumed primacy in the familial order, the natural heir to his kingdom. This romantic ideal dashed, it had been replaced with the harsh reality that he was the seemingly unwanted chattel of his maternal family, the Bishops. As such, he was now subject to the discretions of its patriarch, his uncle, Tom Bishop. In his *Confessions*, there is not a kind word levied toward his uncle, with several paragraphs dedicated to his utter excoriation. Further undermining what stability the young Crowley might have clung to, Tom Bishop convinced his mother to leave the family home in Surrey to be closer to her kin in the nearby suburb of Streatham.

When away at school, things progressively worsened. In an atmosphere where salacious accusation was as good as proof, a gaggle of tattletales hungry to escape the lash is bred, lest they be implicated first. Having visited Crowley at his parent's home over the holidays, one boy returned to school with a tale that he had witnessed young Alick drunk. This was nonsense, but it didn't matter to his particularly vicious headmaster, Reverend Champney. Crowley was placed "in Coventry," a literal ostracism from his teachers and classmates, who were forbidden to interact with him in any way until he confessed the crime and faced the punishment. He refused to do so, being innocent of the crime—ignorant even of the crime for which he had been accused!—and was left in such a state for a term and half, having only bread and water on which to subsist. The result was that the already sickly child developed a severe case of albuminuria, a potentially fatal kidney disease. His family finally intervened and had him removed from the school, which purportedly closed shortly thereafter as the result of complaints from other parents as well.

No small damage had been done: young Alick's health was in shambles, and his doctors predicted he would not live to see adulthood. To counter this diagnosis, he was pulled from school altogether and placed in the care of private tutors and given to travels across Scotland and Wales in the hopes that he might recover his vitality, a prescription that ultimately served him well. His health gradually returned as he spent summers engaged in outdoor activities such as golf, fishing, and mountain climbing—away from the stifling physical and intellectual confines of the boarding school. His newfound freedom was not a complete victory, however, as his tutors were specifically chosen by his uncle under the auspices of what Crowley termed his "extraordinarily narrow, ignorant and bigoted Evangelicalism ... " [5] He spent most of his time arranging ways to outwit them, often with great success. Crowley notes, "These persons ... were not too satisfactory; they were all my Uncle Tom's nominees; that is, they were of the sawny, anaemic, priggish type, ... Of course, I considered it my duty to outwit them in every possible way and hunt up some kind of sin." [6]

A timely savior would come in the guise of Archibald Douglas, after the latest line of tutors had given up on the boy. Not only could Crowley see Douglas as an intellectual equal, but his new tutor would assert to no small relief that the pleasures of the world could be both safely and morally engaged in, provided of course that they did not cross into excess. Douglas's relative moral leniency provided a much-needed breath of fresh air for a young man just then coming into his adulthood, and the "sin" Crowley was all too quick to hunt up was exactly what you might expect of a young man in his later teens—and from the evangelical point of view the most forbidden of fruits! He quips, "Here was certainly a sin worth

5   Crowley, *Confessions*, 54.

6   Ibid., 71.

sinning and I applied myself with characteristic vigour to its practice."[7] The discovery that sex, which until this point had been the most abominable and unmentionable of sins, was something that could be enjoyed and was in fact *enjoyable* was the first of many now seemingly obvious revelations that set the young Crowley on his future path—with the willing assistance of several local girls, of course. Lesser vices such as drinking and smoking quickly fell by the wayside in the wake of his triumph over this greater transgression.

Though it would have a great impact on him, the arrangement with Douglas would be predictably short-lived. As soon as his mother and uncle got wind of Crowley's suspicious sense of happiness, they arrived on the scene and promptly dismissed Crowley's latest tutor. Those who followed would suffer the same fate as those who preceded, either dismissed or dismayed at their inability to control a young man who in retrospect seemed only to have wanted to be treated as an equal.

The remainder of Crowley's school years fortunately found him in good health. This allowed him to return to boarding school, but this time at the less oppressive schools of Malvern and Tonbridge, though still with the occasional tutor to ensure a proper moral upbringing in the view of the Plymouth Brethren. He held the latter school, Tonbridge, in especial regard, largely in part because he had reached an age and fullness of health that prevented a great deal of the bullying he had endured elsewhere. He continued to fill his leisure time with mountain climbing and other outdoor activities critical to maintaining his health, but it seemed that the dark days of his childhood were finally lifting.

Aleister Arrives

In 1895, Crowley entered Trinity College at Cambridge University at the height of his newfound vitality, and shortly thereafter invested himself with the name by which the world would come to know him: *Aleister*. The Gaelic

---

7   Ibid., 71.

derivative of his middle name, he chose it for reasons associated with his literary aspirations, having read that "the most favourable name for becoming famous was one consisting of a dactyl followed by a spondee..." [8] His cousin assured him (incorrectly) that Aleister was the appropriate spelling, rather than the more common rendering of Alaisdair.

The vast sum of his inheritance was now at his disposal, as well, held in trust until he had attained adulthood, and the freedom of university life seems to have suited young Crowley well. He spent his time engaged in the debate club for a time, and excelling in the chess club, famously beating its club president in their first match. However, these were but idle distractions to Crowley's aim of repairing the manifold flaws in his religious education. The sparse reading lists of his puritanical upbringing left large gaps in his knowledge, and he was determined to close them. There were entire classes of literature that needed attending to, and he delved headlong into that endeavor. Crowley spent much of his time reading classics instead of attending to his assigned classwork, importing books "by the ton." [9]

Now far from the oversight of his sternly religious household, he could also more freely engage in the sexual freedoms that he had only so recently discovered. He notes in *Confessions* that "Every woman that I met enabled me to affirm magically that I had defied the tyranny of the Plymouth Brethren." [10] As any individual might, his early and entirely natural sexual appetite was tinged with the hallmark of his individuation: that of rebellion against the experience of his childhood's religious oppression. However, despite the burgeoning poet's own grand gestures toward the concept of romantic idealism, his so-called magical defiance

---

8   Crowley, *Confessions*, 140. (A dactyl is a long syllable followed by two short syllables, while a spondee consists of two long syllables; hence, Ale-is-ter Crow-ley. Crowley, as they say, rhymes with *holy*, the first syllable sounding like the bird of the same name.)

9   Ibid., 115.

10 Ibid., 142.

did not appear to result in any lasting relationships. While he would have encounters with several women, it was in fact a man by the name of Jerome Pollitt (1871–1942)[11] who truly awakened his muse.

Crowley the poet

Slightly older than Crowley, Pollitt, the equally well-to-do son of a newspaper publisher, was pursuing his MA at Cambridge, but was locally notorious as a female impersonator and dancer under the stage

---

11   His full name was Herbert Charles Pollitt; he assumed the name Jerome, much the same as Crowley had assumed Aleister.

name Diane de Rougy.[12] Meeting toward the end of the October term in 1897, he introduced Crowley to the writings of Decadent authors such as Beardsley and Wilde, both of whom were friends. Crowley notes that it was the first "intimate friendship" of his life,[13] but it was of course much more than that. In Pollitt, Crowley would find his first love, and they would spend six months together. To Crowley's eternal regret, it was ultimately his magical aspirations that would cause him to break off the relationship.[14] It was a path that Pollitt simply could not follow, and a path that Crowley was already determined to tread. Ultimately, the severance of the relationship was an unnecessary and rash decision Crowley would regret for the rest of his life. An early volume of Crowley's forlorn poetry was rediscovered in 2014 dating to just after the breakup and with obvious reference to his ex-lover.[15] He notes having seen him once later in life but not having had the courage to approach him.

It was also in this period that he began writing poetry in earnest, his eyes newly open to the greater scope of literature now available to him for inspiration, as opposed to the staid measure of religious verse. He published regularly in the school's student publications,[16] and he also published his first book of poetry, entitled *Aceldama: A Place to Bury Strangers In.* He published this anonymously as "A gentleman of the University of Cambridge" as a nod to one of his more prevalent influences at the time, Percy Bysshe Shelley (1792–1822), who published using a similar phrasing while an undergraduate at Oxford. He would also publish a

---

12   The name was a play on Liane de Pougy, born Anne Marie Chassaigne (1869–1950), a contemporary bisexual French performer and courtesan.

13   Crowley, *Confessions*, 142.

14   It is also fair to state that they had little in common beyond mutual attraction, which set an upper limit on the duration of the relationship. It likely would have ended irrespective of Crowley's growing interest in occultism.

15   Maev Kennedy, "Black Magician Aleister Crowley's Early Gay Verse Comes to Light," 2014.

16   Kaczynski, *Perdurabo*, 35.

compendium of erotic poetry, *White Stains*, under the pen name of George Archibald Bishop in 1898. [17] The last name, Bishop, was certainly a jab at his mother's family—but also British slang for *penis*!

Aside from his schoolwork and poetry, Crowley continued to pursue an interest in mountaineering. He was already a skilled climber, having scaled many of Britain's more difficult peaks, including the chalk cliffs at Beachy Head, once thought unassailable. Time between semesters was now spent climbing more difficult peaks across Europe. Later in life he would make ascents on the Swiss Alps, and even K2, and while he would never make the guarded rolls of the hallowed Alpine Club, it was this passion that led him into contact with men who held connections to another of his interests, and one for which he would ultimately become more famous: magick.

FURTHER READING
The Collected Works of Aleister Crowley
White Stains

The Dawn of the Magician

Karl von Eckartshausen's *The Cloud upon the Sanctuary*, noted in a periodical edited by occult scholar A. E. Waite, particularly caught Crowley's attention. A work of Christian esoteric philosophy, *The Cloud upon the Sanctuary* describes a common theme in Western mystical literature: that our current state, based on ego-perception and rationalization (the cloud), blinds us to the greater internal and spiritual perception that is the true source of all wisdom and intellect (the sanctuary). However, its pronouncement of a school of initiates entrusted with the keys to this arcane science is what truly drew the young Crowley in: " ... a more advanced

---

17   The title alludes to exactly what you think it does. He would also publish the purposely vulgar and comic collection of erotic verse *Snowdrops from a Curate's Garden* in 1904.

school has always existed to whom this deposition of all science has been confided..." [18]

If there was an invisible school of initiates, Crowley was determined to find it.

The key to Crowley's connection was Oscar Eckenstein, a man he met while climbing Wasdale Head during Easter of 1898. Shorter and of sturdier build, Eckenstein was twenty years older and significantly more disciplined in his approach to mountaineering, a welcome mentor to improve on Crowley's self-taught method. Crowley reflected that "His style was invariably clean, orderly and intelligible; mine can hardly be described as human." [19] Crowley was still a self-taught novice by any standard, despite his accomplishments, and he would need greater training and discipline if he were to successfully tackle some of the more treacherous summits he had in mind. He and Eckenstein spent the summer perfecting alpine climbing techniques on the Schonbuhl glacier on the south side of the Dent Blanche in the Swiss Alps.

While poor weather and Crowley's ever-precarious health kept them from accomplishing as much as they had hoped, Crowley had brought ample reading material to pass the time. One of these was *The Kabbalah Unveiled* by S. L. MacGregor Mathers, to which Crowley asserts, "I didn't understand a word of it, but it fascinated me all the more for that reason, and it was my constant study on the glacier." [20] Without yet knowing it, he had encountered his future magical mentor by virtue of that work, as Mathers was at this point the sole head of the Golden Dawn, a working magical order based in London. He appealed to the universe to deliver him a master, and he would soon find one.

Crowley eventually descended from the glacier to recuperate, finding himself in a discussion on alchemy with some of the locals and visiting

---

18   Karl von Eckartshausen's, *The Cloud upon the Sanctuary*, 32.

19   Crowley, *Confessions*, 154.

20   Ibid., 164.

climbers for which the town was a natural base of operations. It was through this conversation that he met Julian Baker, an actual practitioner of alchemy, in contrast to Crowley's theoretical knowledge of the subject. Alas, no search for a master comes easily, and he found that Baker had left when he arose the next morning, precisely when Crowley hoped to press him on the topic of initiation. Crowley pursued, enduring one near miss after another until he finally caught up with Baker ten miles outside of town. After Crowley confided in Baker of his search for a true initiatory school of magick, Baker promised to meet Crowley back in London where he could introduce him to a much greater magician than he. That man was George Cecil Jones, in whom Crowley would find a friend and mentor for many years. Jones was finally someone Crowley could consider a true magician in every respect, and the man that introduced him to the body of initiates he so desperately sought: The Hermetic Order of the Golden Dawn.

Formed as a conjunction of Christian Qabalah, Rosicrucianism, and Freemasonry, and dressed in Egyptian mythology, The Golden Dawn was the principal genius of William Wynn Westcott. [21] Westcott further enlisted his Rosicrucian compatriot, Dr. William Robert Woodman, who had a compatible interest and expertise in Qabalah. However, the strengths of these two men were primarily academic: it was the third individual, S. L. MacGregor Mathers, who would develop this academic knowledge, in concert with his own, into an active initiatory order.

Each of these men were members of the *Societas Rosicruciana in Anglia* (SRIA), itself a Rosicrucian reconstructionist order as the name indicates. Woodman, Westcott, and Mathers expanded the Rosicrucian mystical teachings of the SRIA into a functional magical order by 1888 with the opening of the Isis-Urania Temple in London. The order's initiatory

---

21   The introduction to Israel Regardie's *The Golden Dawn* notes that a Robert Wentworth Little was the original head of the order and passed it to Woodman as early as 1878 (p. 17). However, the organization as it came to be known is generally attributed to the three men described herein.

system was based on a set of "cipher manuscripts" that alleged to show the skeleton of the ritual frameworks, and gave them charter to open the school from certain continental adepts—a claim that is now generally regarded as having been fabricated in an attempt to derive an air of legitimacy for the fledgling cabal. As members worked through the degrees of the order, they would be presented more information surrounding the practice of Western occultism, augmented somewhat liberally with a syncretic mix of Eastern tattwa symbolism, chakras, and similar practices that were then (as today) of fashionable interest to spiritual seekers. In contrast to the Masonic organizations, including the SRIA, to which the men belonged, this order would be open to both men and women, ultimately counting among its membership such luminaries as occult author and historian A. E. Waite, poet W. B. Yeats, and Arthur Machen, an early writer of occult and supernatural horror. By the time Crowley arrived, Woodman had passed, and Westcott had been forced to withdraw, given his public position and political standing as the official coroner for London; his esoteric pursuits were untenable. Mathers was now the last remaining founder and sole head of the Golden Dawn.

The not-yet-famous Aleister Crowley joined the Hermetic Order of the Golden Dawn in 1898, undergoing its *neophyte* initiation ritual in October of that year. One can imagine his excitement upon entering the antechamber of the London temple, finally crossing the threshold of the initiatory brotherhood he had desired to enter for so long. Once arrived, he was instructed to put on the long black robe and red slippers he obtained for the purpose and wait silently. A man dressed in a white robe and holding a scepter would eventually emerge from the western end of the main temple, accompanied by a sentinel in black. Crowley was blindfolded and bound by a rope wrapped three times about his waist before the imposing figure in white knocked once upon the entry door and lead him blindly forward into the adventure he had so fervently sought.

A look at the initial knowledge lectures of the Golden Dawn shows why Crowley's enthusiasm was immediately dampened. For a man that had been seeking a true initiation while studying the depth and breadth of occult writings for several years, being handed "secret" documents that discussed trivial curricula such as the four elements, the seven planets, the twelve signs of the zodiac, and the Hebrew alphabet—all readily available information and certainly well-known by him—left the experience somewhat flat after the exhilaration and grandeur of the admittedly remarkable neophyte initiation.

Not all was lost, however. The Golden Dawn proved exceedingly fruitful in developing Crowley's skill and knowledge in *Qabalah*, a Jewish mystical tradition that had long since been segregated and evolved separately as part of the development of Christian magical practices during the Renaissance. This practice had been at the philosophical heart of ceremonial magick in Europe for centuries, so it is no surprise to find it at the heart of one of the most successful magical orders to date, though further augmented through the extensive associative and comparative symbology of the Order. It ultimately became the framework and symbol-set through which Crowley would express the sublimities of his philosophies and ideas. It is in fact exceedingly difficult to understand Crowley without understanding the Qabalah, as much of his thought process was built on its manifold connections and analogies. Despite his initial disappointments, and with encouragement from Jones and others, he pressed on and quickly attained each of the degrees of the Golden Dawn's instructive outer order by May of the following year.

It was also within the Golden Dawn that he met one of his greatest influences, Allan Bennett. After attending a seasonal ritual at the temple, he was approached by the then-unknown-to-him Bennett, who famously declared, "Little brother, you have been meddling with the *Goetia*!" The *Goetia* is one of the best-known manuscripts on conjuring evil spirits, and Crowley denied it, prompting Bennett's response, "Then the *Goetia* has been meddling with you!" Crowley, of course, *had* been meddling with the *Goetia*, and he and Bennett would soon become fast friends. It was equally rumored, with reasonable cause, that they were lovers.

Crowley would rent two rooms, one for himself and the other for the impoverished Bennett, arranged such that the two could study magick together—Bennett being the more experienced of the two. Like Crowley, Bennett was also an asthmatic and cycled through a number of medicines to help him maintain his health. Given that this was turn-of-the-twentieth-century prescription medicine, this meant cocaine and opiates, among others, all of which were commonly available through a physician if not simply purchased over the counter. Thus, along with experiments with more traditional magical practices, they began experimenting with drug-induced states of altered consciousness as well. This was much more than simple drug use: it was true experimentation in the vein of Huxley, methodical and precise, and a systematic study that Crowley pursued throughout his life. Fitting with how they first met, Bennett and Crowley soon used *Goetia* to speed the ailing Bennett to the warmer climates of Ceylon, now known as Sri Lanka, in order to combat his worsening asthma.

Coincidental with the departure of his friend and mentor, however, he would find that the Order to which he had pledged his hopes was starting to come undone. S. L. MacGregor Mathers recused himself to Paris, leaving the confines of the London temples of the Golden Dawn in order to further establish his relationship with the "Secret Chiefs" and advance the higher degrees of the Order. This left London in the hands of higher adepts that did not look as favorably or leniently on Crowley's lifestyle, especially the rumors of his homosexuality. It is possible that jealousy of Mathers's new star pupil had an influence, as well. When Crowley applied to the London office for his due advancement to the inner order of the Golden Dawn, he was denied. No reasons were given. He was simply not the sort of person that the London initiates wanted to be associated with.

Undaunted, Crowley again left for Paris, where upon petition Mathers conferred to him the degree he sought, admitting him to ranks of the Second Order. This was where Crowley had been told the real secrets were kept, the very magical secrets he had pursued since his days at Cambridge. Returning to London, he demanded the papers to which he was now entitled, but was once more rebuffed. The Order was splintering along the lines of Mathers's authority in London and speculation about the validity of the famed cipher documents that purported to give the Order legitimacy in the first place. A bitter fight would ensue, effectively destroying the Golden Dawn until it was resurrected some decades later, but Crowley was on his way.

FURTHER READING

The Cloud upon the Sanctuary by Karl von Eckartshausen

The Golden Dawn by Israel Regardie

The Mystical Qabalah by Dion Fortune

The Goetia by Aleister Crowley

Mr. & Mrs. Crowley

Crowley met a young Gerald Kelly at Cambridge in May of 1898 after the latter had picked up a copy of his poem *Aceldama* and determined to meet the author based on his "Gentleman of the University of Cambridge" homage, being an admirer of Shelley as well. They would strike up a strong friendship that endured for a great many years, but most importantly it was through his new friend that he would meet Kelly's sister Rose, his future wife.

Crowley's wife, Rose Kelly

Crowley had returned to his recently purchased highland estate, Bole-skine, on the shores of Loch Ness in Scotland after spending some time on the European continent. He received word that Gerald would be visiting nearby, along with his mother, his sister, and her fiancé, and he naturally rushed to meet him. Finding himself alone with Gerald's sister Rose while the other men played golf, having not brought his clubs, Rose confessed that although she was betrothed, she did not love her fiancé—nor the *other* man that she had agreed to marry! Moreover, she was in love with *yet another* man who was already married, but her parents were insisting she marry one of her two suitors. It did not take long for Crowley to determine the obvious course of action: to avoid such a loveless fate, she should marry *him*! As a marriage of convenience, she would then be free to take up the residence the (married) man she loved had set aside for her without further interference. Gerald, when told, naturally thought their outlandish scheme was a joke.

That same day, Crowley enquired of the local parish priest as to whether they could be married on the spot, a request the clergyman flatly rejected on the feeble grounds that they would not be able to publish the marriage banns—public announcements of the wedding. When Crowley pressed—which is to say, "pressed a shilling into his hand"—the priest admitted that the town constable could make all the arrangements without delay. Rising early the next day, the two made it into town at the break of dawn, only to be told that the sheriff might not be available until ten o'clock or later. This was not going to suffice given the required expediency, and so they were directed to a local lawyer instead. Thus, on August 12, 1903, the two became legally married just before Rose's brother Gerald broke through the door in a flurry of fists. Her brother, and in fact her whole family, was incensed and tried to have it annulled, but unfortunately for them it was all perfectly legal. The two set out on their "honeymoon" shortly thereafter to a small resort town in Scotland to give everything an air of legitimacy, though neither at that time considered the arrangement anything more than a measure of expediency. However, by the time they returned, both found themselves in love with the other, and if the start of their relationship was surrounded with such drama, things were only going to get more interesting.

Left to right: Rose, Lola (daughter),
and Crowley, circa 1910

The Equinox of the Gods

Now in love, and ever the romantic idealist, Crowley soon designed a honeymoon tour more befitting of their status, one that would take them to Italy and Cairo before continuing to Ceylon (modern Sri Lanka) and China. By late January, they made their way back to Cairo by way of Suez and Port Said, arriving in Cairo on the ninth of February before moving on to the health resorts of Helwan to the south and registering under the assumed names of *Choia Khan* and *Ouarda*, meaning "The Great Beast" and "Rose" in Hebrew and Arabic, respectively. [22] He was amused at his

---

22   *Choia* is Hebrew for "beast." The title of *khan* is an honorific that can mean anything from "leader" to "king," so it was likely this term to which he turned in
approximating "great"—i.e., exalted, etc., though he never mentions so directly.

obviously fake name, but he was equally interested in studying Islam from within, as Burton [23] had done. He notes, " ... I got a sheikh to teach me Arabic and the practices of ablution, prayer, and so on, so that at some future time I might pass for a Moslem amongst themselves. I had it in mind to repeat Burton's journey to Mecca sooner or later." [24]

Now almost certain of it, the couple suspected that Rose was pregnant, and Boleskine was cold and dreary in the midst of the Scottish winter. Why not wait a month or two until the weather improved? The fair weather of the highlands would arrive just as the heat of Cairo became unbearable, so the decision to stay seemed obvious. (Despite its reputation for sub-standard sanitation, Cairo remained recommended for its desert climate and a fashionable place for the European elite to winter, especially those with breathing problems like the asthmatic Crowley.) Leaving Helwan on or about the twelfth of March, they returned north to Cairo proper and rented a furnished ground-floor apartment near the Boulak Museum in a quarter Crowley described as "fashionably European." [25]

Despite being "weary of Mysticism and dissatisfied with Magick," [26] on March 16, the couple took occasion to visit the pyramids and for Crowley to demonstrate some of the magical practices that he had learned, endeavoring to show his bride the sylphs—elemental spirits of the air—in the King's Chamber of the Great Pyramid at Giza. To Crowley's account, the conjuration was a stunning success, illuminating the chamber by the light of his invocation, but it had a very curious aftereffect. Rose could not see the elemental spirits, but she became hysterical, saying, "They are waiting for you!" Crowley had no idea what she meant.

The following day, he repeated the same invocation, and she persisted, saying, "It is all about the child" and "All Osiris." Half annoyed

---

23   Sir Richard Francis Burton, the British explorer (1821–1890).

24   Crowley, *Confessions*, 388.

25   Crowley, *The Equinox of the Gods*, 109.

26   Ibid., 109–110.

and half intrigued, he determined to sort out this conundrum by invoking the Egyptian god of knowledge, Thoth, for more insight. This invocation was successful, and he made a note that "Thoth, with great success, indwells us." [27] However, for his efforts, he seems to have received no further illumination on the matter, nor indication of the purpose of Rose's continued insistence.

He turned his focus back to Rose the following day, and decided to determine whether her visions were some form of hysteria due to her pregnancy or, alternately, the effects of alcohol. [28] She responded by saying that Crowley had offended the Egyptian god Horus, and that it was this deity attempting to contact him. How could she know this? How could she even know the *name* Horus, unless she had picked it up somehow at random while in the city? Skeptical, he put a number of very technical questions to her regarding the identity of whom she was in contact with, questions that she could not know given a lack of education in both Egyptology and magical practice, much less the attributions defined by the Golden Dawn on which Crowley was to rely.

Crowley asked first about the god's nature, "What are his moral qualities?"

"Force and fire," she replied, correctly.

"What conditions are caused by his presence?"

"A deep blue light," she said. Again, correct, but equally plausible for a number of others.

Crowley had yet to reveal that he had determined the god to be Horus, so he wrote that name amidst a number of others chosen at random. "Pick a name."

She pointed to Horus, the same god that had been indicated to Crowley. "Who is his enemy?"

---

27   Crowley, *The Equinox of the Gods*, 70.

28   The effects of fetal alcohol syndrome were not yet known, so it was relatively common for women at the time to drink throughout their pregnancies.

She answered, "The forces of the water ... of the Nile."

Remarkable. Set, the brother and murderer of his brother Osiris, was the Nile god who was ultimately avenged by Horus!

Still, more technical questions were offered. He asked about his lineal figure and color, and she responded correctly, a probability of eighty-four to one. She answered his place in the temple of the Golden Dawn. She picked the magical weapon with which he was associated from a list of six, his planetary nature from a list of the seven ancient planets, his principal number (one through ten), and from a number of arbitrary symbols. In total, absent the open-ended questions where the odds were impossible to calculate, roughly half of them, she had answered each perfectly, with Crowley estimating the odds at no less than *twenty-one million to one against*. He was forced to take notice.

As a final test, Crowley ventured to take Rose to the museum, where she had yet to visit, so that she could show him an image of the god she claimed to see. Still skeptical, Crowley found himself amused when she walked past several depictions of Horus, and began their journey to the second floor of the museum. In the distance was a glass case, which she pointed to. "There! There he is!" Rushing forward, as the contents were too far away to see with any clarity, he was dumbfounded when in the case stood an image of Horus in the form of Ra-Hoor-Khuit, an amalgamation of that god and the principal solar god Ra, on a wooden funeral *stele* [29] of the Twenty-sixth Dynasty for the priest Ankh-af-na-Khonsu—in an exhibit numbered six hundred and sixty-six, no less! One would think that The Beast had found his calling, but his *Confessions* depicts otherwise, noting that he "dismissed it as an obvious coincidence." [30] This new calling was at odds, after all, with his stubborn and professed disillusionment with magick.

---

29   In archeology, a *stele* or *stela* is a commemorative funerary plaque, column, or block much like a gravestone is used today.

30   Crowley, *Confessions*, 394.

Nonetheless, on March 19, he prepared an invocation and recited it under instructions from Rose, instructions that went against every ounce of magical training he had ever encountered. Wearing a white robe and opening the windows of his ground-floor apartment at half past noon into the streets of the bustling city, he proceeded to shout his invocation of the god Horus into the bustling throngs of people making their way through the crowds of mid-day Cairo. The invocation was met with little success, but he was now less resistant to the idea than before. Perhaps being understandably self-conscious, he asked whether he might manage the invocation at night, which was begrudgingly accepted by Rose and the ethereal voice that guided her. On March 20, at midnight, he began anew, and this time his invocation was a success, with Crowley learning that the "Equinox of the Gods" had begun—a time of massive cultural transition from the paternal age of Osiris, characterized by the major religious themes of the preceding two thousand years, to that of the individualistic Crowned and Conquering Child, and son of Osiris, Horus. As the ritual concluded on the spring equinox and start of the astrological new year, Crowley found himself with a monumental task: "I am to formulate a new link of an Order with the Solar Force." [31] But how? What did that mean?

In the following weeks, Crowley had the verses of the stele translated into French by the assistant curator at the museum, a translation he would later interpret into English poetic verse. He would also work through various Qabalistic analyses of the information he had gathered so far. Finally, on April 7, Rose told Crowley to enter the room they had been using as a temple for the next three successive days and write down what he would hear. No longer permitted to be the skeptic given the events of the last three weeks, Crowley did as he was told. He notes: "I went into the 'temple' a minute early, so as to shut the door and sit down on the stroke of Noon. On my table were my pen—a Swan Fountain—and

---

31   Crowley, *The Equinox of the Gods*, 76.

supplies of Quarto typewriting paper, 8" × 10". I never looked round in the room at any time." [32]

At the stroke of noon, he heard the voice of Aiwass, the "praeternatural entity" that Rose had indicated, who then dictated *The Book of the Law*. The voice came from behind his left shoulder and possessed a "deep timbre, musical and expressive, its tones solemn, voluptuous, tender, fierce or aught else as suited to the moods of the message. Not bass—perhaps a rich tenor or baritone." [33] It began, as Crowley rushed to keep pen to paper, "Had! The manifestation of Nuit. The unveiling of the company of Heaven. Every man and every woman is a star … " [34] The pace was hurried, as evidenced by the writing and volume inscribed within the span of a single hour, and so it would be over the course of the three days.

The result of his efforts would be *The Book of the Law*, [35] a three-chapter text spanning sixty-five handwritten pages that Crowley (and many others) claimed were much more than simple automatic writing. The myriad complexities of the work are too great to enter into here, or arguably anywhere, but at heart it presented a new spiritual law for humanity. An inversion of the prior age, where suffering and deprivation were the key to spiritual attainment, this law was markedly individualist. Its central tenet was "Do what thou wilt," which was not a call to hedonism, but rather a call to personal accountability in the establishment of—and adherence to—one's own moral code. Coupled with intricate esoteric puzzles in support of its authenticity, this book would come to dominate the remainder of Crowley's life and spiritual teachings … after a spell.

With all of the events leading up to the reception of *The Book of the Law*, as well as the circumstances in its *actual* reception, one would think

---

32   Crowley, *The Equinox of the Gods*, 117.

33   Ibid.

34   Crowley, *The Book of the Law*, 1:1–3.

35   Originally titled "Liber L vel Legis sub figura CCXX as delivered by LXXVII to DCLXVI." He would later change the title to *Liber AL vel Legis*.

that Crowley might have taken a stronger and more immediate interest in its study and exegesis. However, Crowley was still quite stubbornly done with magick, having only a passing interest in the practice of *raja yoga*. While he spent some initial effort in the thought of announcing the work, after his ultimate disappointment in Mathers and the Golden Dawn to deliver the initiatory experience he so desperately sought, he was burned out. His plans were to travel, climb mountains, and otherwise spend his days at Boleskine as a man of leisure, and his mind was set to it. It would be some time yet before Crowley stumbled across the manuscript again while retrieving a pair of skis from his attic, but this time his curiosity would hold—and his adventure would begin in earnest.

FURTHER READING

The Book of the Law
The Equinox of the Gods

The Magus and the Equinox

Now back at Boleskine, the Crowleys' only work, aside from the arrangement of some publishing matters, was to await the birth of their child, and so it was that on July 28, 1904, a baby girl by the name Nuit Ma Ahathoor Hecate Sappho Jezebel Lilith Crowley was born. She would go by Lilith for short, and Crowley would find himself truly at home in the Scottish Highlands of Boleskine. The Cairo experience set aside, he notes, "I was bitterly opposed to the principles of *The Book* [of the Law] on almost every point of morality. The third chapter seemed to me gratuitously atrocious." [36]

His other publishing efforts went into full swing, however, taking back his stock from what he believed was the underperforming sales of his present bookseller into his own hands and new imprint: The Society for the Propagation of Religious Truth. "My responsibility to the gods

---

36   Crowley, *Confessions*, 403.

was to write as I was inspired; my responsibility to mankind was to publish what I wrote." [37] It was through this new label that he would release some of his most compelling early works, including among others his well received *The Sword of Song*, his *Collected Works* of poetry to date (in three volumes!), and his edition of the infamous grimoire *Goetia*, which he had collected from the offices of the Golden Dawn some years ago during that dramatic period. [38]

Though he counted these days as extremely happy, the arrival of one of his former climbing associates as a guest of the house brought back a reverie of the misfortunes of his failed attempt on K2. Crowley would be convinced to join an expedition to summit the third highest mountain in the world, Kangchenjunga, high in the Himalayas and as yet unconquered. (His friend and mentor Oscar Eckenstein declined to join the party.) It was already April, however, which meant the assault would need to come together quickly, if not immediately. Crowley departed for the excursion on May 6, just two weeks after his friend's visit, leaving wife and child behind with the family and attendant nurses.

While the preparations came together as well as might be expected given the expediency, the expedition up the mountain proved disastrous— and for an unlucky few, deadly. Striking out from the local village at the base of the mountains in late August, Crowley led their ascent across the treacherous glacial terrain, but by their fourth base camp at nearly twenty thousand feet, the porters were already deserting—another falling to his death as he chose to go off by himself. The party itself appears to have been composed of too many inexperienced climbers for the sort of ascent they were attempting, with logistical difficulties throughout their climb as well, which can prove the untimely end of a climbing party in and of itself.

---

37   Crowley, *Confessions*, 406.

38   While known as a treatise on conjuring evil spirits, Crowley found in it an exceptionally versatile method of invocation for spirits of any type.

Crowley (center) and company on the ill-fated expedition

On the first of September, disaster struck in the form of a small avalanche, not uncommon on the mountain, and something they had already encountered. However, this time, the loose and fast-moving snow took with it a principal member of their party, Alexis Pache, as well as three of their porters. Two other members of the team, Tartarin and de Righi, were also injured in the accident, and it was clear that they could not, or would not, go on. Though surpassing twenty-two thousand vertical feet of the total twenty-eight thousand, the deadly slopes of Kangchenjunga would have their way, and Crowley and his expedition never set foot upon its peak. The expedition was broken, and they had little recourse but to descend the mountain. A cairn, known even today as "Pache's grave," was erected at the base camp on the Yulong glacier in memoriam. The mountain would not be bested for another fifty years.

Dejected, Crowley departed the shadow of the mountain for Rangoon, in what is now Myanmar, and then on to travels across South Asia, where Rose and young Lilith joined him through the end of the winter. While the travel was often rough and inhospitable compared to travels in Europe, the three appear to have traveled quite well, eventually making their way to the port of Hai Phong on the Gulf of Tonkin, some forty miles east of Hanoi, Vietnam. There, after a brief stay, they boarded a ship for Hong Kong, where they decided to travel homeward by different routes: Rose, now pregnant once more, through India to pick up some of their belongings, and Crowley across the Pacific and through North America, sailing on April 21, 1906. Landing in Vancouver, British Columbia, some twelve days later, he remarked at the time that it presented "...no interest to the casual visitor." [39] He traveled across lower Canada through Calgary and Toronto, then crossed into the United States at Niagara to see the Falls and New York City. Ten days in the great metropolis was plenty, and so he set sail for England, arriving in Bournemouth where his mail awaited with devastating news: his daughter Lilith was dead, having caught typhoid fever during the return trip with Rose. [40] Crowley suffered further misfortunes with his health for the remainder of the year, including several operations of varying success. He remained bedridden for much of the last part of the year, which in its own way rekindled his interest in magick: he put down the set of correspondences he had learned in the Golden Dawn, greatly expanding it with his own researches, resulting in his classic *Liber 777*, though that work would not be released for another two years' time.

During his travels across Asia following the climbing expedition, he re-engaged with magical practice and made consistent progress. He also

39   Crowley, *Confessions*, 502.

40   One of his acquaintances callously quipped that she died of "acute nomenclature"—too many names.

became impressed with the idea that his spate of misfortunes resulted from ignoring the task of delivering on the promise of *The Book of the Law* and for not taking up the task that the gods had set before him. He therefore set before himself the task of undertaking the Abramelin Operation once more, repeating his oath before his old friend George Cecil Jones to attain the Knowledge and Conversation of his Holy Guardian Angel, culminating in mid-October of that year.

While the latter half of 1906 was difficult for Crowley, Rose had gone from bad to worse. Likely spurned by the loss of her child, and doubtless aided by her husband's consistent absences, she took to drinking heavily. Their second child, another girl whom they named Lola Zaza, was born premature as a result and barely moved for the first few days of her life, despite the care of their doctors. Crowley notes that he learned his wife purchased 150 bottles of whiskey in just five months—and that was just from *one* of the grocers. She agreed to counseling, but it did not stick, and she was back to heavy drinking within a fortnight, making their relationship impossible. They ultimately divorced in 1909, though they remained in contact, even being photographed together shortly after the final divorce decree. Crowley could no longer be responsible for her self-destruction, and unabated, she was committed to an asylum in 1911. They would not reunite before her death in 1932.

The marriage now passed, Crowley understood that his reception of *The Book of the Law* placed him in a unique position to reformulate magick on the grounds of a New Aeon, but he had much work to do in order to lay a legitimate claim. To advance his work, he had to complete the task for which Mathers had left England: to make contact with the "Secret Chiefs," the invisible adepts he believed had forever guided humanity toward enlightenment. His prior work had prepared him well, and he had begun taking in students.

The dissolution of the Golden Dawn had left a vacuum for those seekers interested in the initiatory systems of magick and mysticism that

Crowley had become so intimately acquainted with, and Crowley found himself with a renewed vigor to carry out the work that he had so long set himself to. As a vehicle for those teachings, he determined to create the magical order that he had sought in joining the Golden Dawn, expressed so captivatingly in Eckartshausen's *The Cloud upon the Sanctuary*. This order would be called the *Argenteum Astrum* (A∴ A∴), Latin for Silver Star.

The A∴ A∴ was announced through a new subscription-based periodical of Crowley's own design, entitled *The Equinox*. It was offered on the equinoxes of each year and contained a number of articles, short stories, and allegorical poems. Its initial release in the spring of 1909 also contained all the previously unpublished Golden Dawn rituals in Crowley's possession, his way of cementing the demise of that organization and his former mentor, Mathers, by removing the veils of its secrecy. The publication of these rituals ultimately lead to a very public lawsuit between the two men in which Crowley emerged victorious. *The Equinox* continued with increased publicity from news coverage of the trial, with the tenth and final number in the first volume being issued in the fall of 1913.

Despite the tragedies he endured, this was an exceptionally fertile period for Crowley, writing not only the bulk of *Equinox*, but many inspired works that would be issued later as the three volumes of *Thelema*, now commonly referenced as *The Holy Books of Thelema*. Written between 1907 and 1911 while in a state of ecstatic trance, these works were intended to transmit the Logos of the Aeon, the essential spiritual concepts of Thelema. While *The Book of the Law* holds an especial place within the scope of these works, the remaining holy books may be considered equally enlightening, and he included them as required reading in his curriculum for the A∴ A∴. Crowley especially favored *Liber Cordis Cincti Serpente* and *Liber Liberi vel Lapidis Lazuli*, assigning them as required reading in two of the earliest grades in his fledgling order.

FURTHER READING

The Holy Books of Thelema

The Equinox, Volume 1, Numbers 1–10

The Temple of the East

While the publicity from the trial against Mathers over *The Equinox* brought him into contact with several esoteric groups claiming (or seeking) authority in such matters, he claims to have turned them all away. The initial surge of those interested would soon ebb to a predictable trickle of new membership. However, Crowley had established a set of London offices for the publication, and thereby the Order, through which he met his next "Scarlet Woman," a term he adopted for his sex magick partners to compliment his identification as The Beast. This was Australian violinist Leila Waddell, to whom he referred as *Laylah*, meaning "night" in both Arabic and Hebrew.

Arguably one of Crowley's most profound works, *The Book of Lies* was published in 1912, containing ninety-three short mystical aphorisms—the first chapter consisting merely of a question mark and an exclamation point. The book was so named because that which could be communicated was in and of itself subject to both the bias of the communicator and the bias of the communicant with respect to their relative, subjective experiences. Hence, anything he could write on such mystical subjects was inherently corrupted by the limitations of language and its inability to adequately communicate meaning. The text stated the only thing that could be believed of *The Book of Lies* was its imprint date, which of course was deliberately incorrect, stating 1913 rather than 1912.

The individual chapters vary greatly in both content and length, but nothing longer than a page or two. Chapters 25 and 36 show Crowley's early revisions of the Golden Dawn pentagram and hexagram rituals as the Star Ruby and Star Sapphire, respectively, those chapter numbers being the squares of five and six. Chapter 69, "The Way to Succeed—and the Way to Suck Eggs!" requires a note that it can only be deciphered by experts in English puns, where the entire chapter alludes outwardly to oral sex and yet still inwardly to a profound note on the practice of sex magick. Chapter 77, bearing the same number as the Hebrew word for goat, OZ, contains nothing but the word "Laylah," also enumerating to 77, and a picture of Leila Waddell, nude from the waist up, with her long black hair covering her breasts—all of which may be connected with the idea of the Sabbatic Goat of witches' lore. He notes in his *Confessions* that *The Book of Lies* represented a "compendium of the contents of my consciousness," [41] and those contents would bring an interesting knock on Crowley's door not soon after publication.

"You have published the secret!" declared the native German from under his thick mustache. The man at the door was none other than Theodor Reuss, the head of the Ordo Templi Orientis, a Masonic order whose higher degree rituals encoded specific instructions on sexual magick. [42] Crowley was incredulous, or so he claims, and declared he had done no such thing. Undaunted, Reuss pulled out a copy of *The Book of Lies* and rifled through its pages until he found chapter 36, titled "The Star Sapphire." Confronted with its overtly sexual symbolism, which speaks in veiled allegory about a sexual act in describing "the real and perfect Ritual of the Hexagram," [43] Crowley was taken aback. He was not surprised by the sexuality, which was quite intentional, but the idea that it spoke to the underlying symbolism of all Masonry had not occurred to him. "It

---

41   Crowley, *Confessions*, 687.

42   Some accounts have Crowley initially joining the O.T.O. in 1910, shortly after his legal battle with Mathers over publishing the Golden Dawn materials, only being elevated to the IX° after the publication of *The Book of Lies*. The exact timelines are unclear, and perhaps deliberately so, but Crowley does note he was acquainted with Reuss by late 1910.

43   Crowley, *The Book of Lies*, 83. Due to publication restrictions by the British government concerning sexually explicit material, Crowley had to avoid any direct mention of sex in any of his work, typically hiding it under the guise of being "for initiates" or through purposely absurd analogies.

instantly flashed upon me. The entire symbolism, not only of freemasonry but of many other traditions, blazed upon my spiritual vision. From that moment, the O.T.O. assumed its proper importance in my mind." [44]

Thus began Crowley's involvement in Ordo Templi Orientis. Originally envisioned as an initiatory school for high-ranking Masons, its teachings regarding the secrets of sexual magick became a practice with which Crowley became nearly synonymous. His discussions with Reuss lead Crowley to join the Order and eventually preside over all English-speaking countries during Reuss's lifetime. Crowley soon set himself to work in reforming the rituals of the O.T.O. along Thelemic lines, producing what is considered by many initiates of that order to be Crowley's true masterwork and legacy. He assumed full responsibility for the Order after Reuss's death in 1923.

Along with the O.T.O., Reuss also had authority in *L'Église Catholique Gnostique*, the Gnostic Catholic Church. Founded in France in 1907 as an offshoot of an earlier incarnation founded by Jules Doinel, the church was established by Jean Bricaud, Louis-Sophrone Fugairon, and Gérard Encausse, the latter of whom wrote a number of esoteric works more famously under the name Papus. At a 1908 conference for Spiritualist Masonic orders organized by Encausse, he and Reuss would exchange rights for Reuss to operate within *L'Église Catholique Gnostique* and Encausse to have authority in Reuss's Masonic *Rites of Memphis and Mizraim*. Reuss collected this religious organization into the catalogue of his own O.T.O.

Unsurprisingly, the underlying theological foundation of *L'Église Catholique Gnostique* was decidedly Christian, which of course would not do for Crowley. With authority over the church by virtue of his position in O.T.O., Crowley first wrote and then installed his own Gnostic Mass as "the central public and private ritual of the O.T.O." and renamed the church after the Latin equivalent: *Ecclesia Gnostica Catholica* (E.G.C.).

---

44   Crowley, *Confessions*, 710.

Crowley in Masonic regalia

Written in 1913 while in Moscow, the Gnostic Mass provides a symbolic representation in ritual form of the O.T.O.'s innermost secret in Thelemic symbolism, the same secret that brought Reuss knocking on Crowley's door a year earlier following the publication of *The Book of Lies*. The Gnostic Mass is now performed under the auspices of the E.G.C. by O.T.O. bodies around the world.

FURTHER READING

The Book of Lies

The Gnostic Mass

The Great War and the Great Work

"...I cannot but conclude that at least for a long period anarchy will triumph in Europe." [45]

When Archduke Ferdinand was assassinated on June 28, 1914, it sparked a domino effect of treaty alliances drawn up for and against one country and another that would ultimately lead to the advent of the Great War, embroiling nearly every developed nation into a conflict that resulted in over thirty-eight million casualties, including seventeen million deaths. Crowley was disgusted, later referring to it as "the culmination of [Europe's] many centuries of corruption by Christianity," [46] and citing cheap newspapers as having turned his countrymen into a hysterical mob. His native England was of course deeply involved, and despite his distaste for the circumstances that brought it about, Crowley was determined to help. To his mind, he was, first and foremost, an English gentleman, bound by honor to king and country. He made several attempts to contact the British government with offers of his service, none of which bore fruit. His reputation as both an eccentric magician and all the resultant salacious press surrounding his earlier court trials (and likely his suspect homosexuality) preceded him, and an attack of phlebitis—inflammation of the veins caused by blood clots—made impossible any more strenuous duties for the man now approaching forty. He would lament that "My leg and my Sunday School record alike" would conspire to keep him out of the war effort directly. [47]

That desire dashed, Crowley instead set his sails for America on an invitation to New York, sailing on the Lusitania, the same ship sunk by German U-boats in May of the following year, which served as an initial catalyst for America's eventual entry into the Great War. He hoped to sell some of his publications to a wealthy collector, but when there was a delay

---

45   Crowley, *Confessions*, 727.

46   Crowley, *Confessions*, 726.

47   Crowley, *Confessions*, 744.

in receiving his shipped works, he found himself with a little time to spare. While on a bus traveling through New York's glitzy Fifth Avenue in early 1915, described as "a sort of ditch lined with diamonds and over-rouged stenographers,"[48] he was approached by a man enquiring of his views on Germany and Austria. Not wanting to tip his hand either way, he replied in relative sympathy, and was given a card that led to the offices of *The Fatherland*, a German propaganda paper run by George Viereck.

Seeing an opportunity to serve his country after all, Crowley played the sympathizer to the German cause with the angle of an Irish rebel and began writing for *The Fatherland*. The Sinn Fein movement had formed in opposition to Britain and provided the perfect cover of Irish nationalism under which Crowley could operate, tracing his own name back to Irish ancestry from O'Crowley and de Quérouaille. True to form, he made a show of it, burning an envelope purported to contain his British passport before the Statue of Liberty, thereafter hoisting the Irish flag while a violinist played "The Wearing of the Green." The spectacle would end up in *The New York Times*, along with the expected coverage in *The Fatherland*.

Crowley would begin writing ostensibly pro-German propaganda, but while his initial offerings were somewhat staid, his prose gradually gave way to the most lurid fanaticism designed to make the cause look patently absurd. While it would be an exceptional hyperbole to suggest that Crowley was the cause of America's entering the war, natural alliances and German use of unrestricted submarine warfare serving well enough to sway the public, it is interesting to note he had a part in hampering the German propaganda efforts in New York, one of the largest German population centers in America. While not officially sanctioned, he did have a friend in British Naval Intelligence who was aware of his work, and he would find his eventual repatriation curiously unobstructed.

While in New York, he also met popular astrologer Evangeline Adams, a distant relative of the former US presidents of the same name,

---

48 Crowley, *Confessions*, 746.

who had made her own name through a very lucrative mail-order astrology business. Defending her practice in a number of court cases against accusations of fraudulent practice, she was successful in all of them, paving the way for much of modern-day popular astrology—even to the publication of daily horoscopes in the papers. Among the nation's elite, she would count among her clientele such notable persons as financier J. P. Morgan. There was only one trouble: as far as Crowley could tell, she had no idea how astrology worked at all.

Crowley agreed to ghostwrite a work on astrology for Adams, with his own idea to set astrology on a firm and rational scientific basis firmly in mind. He was still writing false propaganda pieces for *The Fatherland* as well as lighter articles and poetry for *Vanity Fair*, but as time passed he'd made less progress than he had hoped on Adams's work. When the attractions of the city were found to be too distracting to make significant progress, at least from Adams's perspective, she offered Crowley the use of her cabin on the secluded shores of Newfound Lake in Bristol, New Hampshire. [49] Traveling by train from New York, he arrived in mid-July of 1916, bringing with him a canoe and small axe "to remind him of George Washington," [50] and a small amount of both ether and mescaline—readily and legally available from the right chemist at the time.

Crowley stayed in the small cottage by the lake through the summer and into the fall when much of the resort town shuttered, as is common for the off-season period. Sitting at the base of what is now the White Mountain National Forest, and fed therefrom, the lake is quite cold even in the summer! To Crowley, however, it was a much needed respite and "magical retirement." Ironically, upon reaching the shores of the wooded resort town, he recognized that the Adams work was a distraction from

---

49   Crowley referred to the lake as "Lake Pasquaney," which stems from a popular attempt among locals to rename the lake after what they understood as its original Native American name. It never took root, however, and it remains New-found Lake to this day.

50   Crowley, "The Elixer of Life: Our Magical Medicine," *Amrita*, 12.

those very personal aims he had dedicated himself to, and he would all but abandon the project. Despite their eventual split over the finances, Evangeline Adams ultimately published two books based on Crowley's input, *Astrology: Your Place in the Sun* (1927) and *Astrology: Your Place Among the Stars* (1930). An earlier manuscript of Crowley's work has since been published under the title *The General Principles of Astrology* (2002).

More importantly, Crowley was working through a deeply personal initiatory phase in his life, begun in New York, which he dubbed "Chokmah Days" after a sphere on the Qabalistic Tree of Life, meaning "wisdom." Chokmah is the sphere related to the attainment of the Grade of the Magus, where the individual becomes inexorably identified with the utterance of his *logos*, a Greek term meaning "word," and in this context implying a spiritual truth. (To the Buddha, that *logos* was Anatta, or *without-soul*, which upended its theological predecessors, for example.) While Crowley had worked hard to accept *The Book of the Law* and his position in having received it, to completely give himself over to its exposition and promulgation was another step altogether. More than simply giving his ego over to the pursuit of this cause, he now sought to become the personification of the *logos*, of Thelema. We can only speculate whether Crowley reflected on his religious upbringing in Christ's utterance and identification with "the way and the life," as well, though he did think to mock-crucify a frog before serving it up as frog's legs for dinner! It was his way of banishing the preceding aeon's slavish adherence to the formula of the dying god, now abrogated. By the time he arrived in San Francisco later that year, Crowley had attained this goal and began introducing himself with the phrase with which the world would associate him, "Do what thou wilt shall be the whole of the Law." And so he would until the end of his days.

Leaving New Hampshire as the autumn leaves fell, he spent time in New York City, New Orleans, and Detroit, to name but a few, as well as making a tour of the West Coast from Vancouver, British Columbia, to

San Francisco, California. In some places, such as in Detroit, his visits brought the same sort of salacious press coverage he had come to expect at home, but in others he remained just another—albeit somewhat eccentric—British expatriate. By late 1919, the war in Europe now having ended, Crowley was ready to go home.

FURTHER READING

The General Principles of Astrology by Crowley and Adams

The Abbey

While he had made great spiritual progress during his time in America, Crowley's return to England following the war was less a triumphant homecoming than a resounding defeat on nearly all fronts. His work for *The Fatherland* may have been tolerated and even understood by the British government as the act of sabotage it was, but the British populace was naturally unaware of the activities of British Intelligence, much less a saboteur working under no official guidance. They saw only his published work and viewed him as a traitor. In retaliation, police had raided the London offices of the O.T.O., and the Order had been forced to sell off Boleskine for funds, Crowley having invested the property in the Order prior to his departure as a means of attracting new membership with its many amenities. He returned penniless and homeless, the material manifestations of his magical work in tatters.

Undeterred, and given his newfound (albeit compelled) lack of attachments, he considered his identification with the Law of Thelema and struck upon the idea that he should create a community along Thelemic lines where aspirants from across the world could gather and pursue their own spiritual enlightenment. Consulting the *I Ching*, as he often did in times such as this, the oracle pointed to a small town on the Sicilian coast: Cefalu. Yet, these were troubling times on the continent, and Crowley found himself arriving in Rome on the very day of the fascist Mussolini's *coup d'état* and consolidation of his power as *Il Duce*. The fullness of that terrible history having yet to be written, he moved on by train from the events in the capital city to the coast, and across the blue waters of the Mediterranean to the island of Sicily. The town of Cefalu itself lay in the center of the northern coast of that island, known in ancient times as Cephaloedium, its rustic villas nestled amongst the jagged rock formations that soar out of the beautiful ocean waters below. Thought to have once been a fortress, one considers the location's resemblance to the opening stanzas of the third chapter of *The Book of the Law*, "Choose ye an island! Fortify it! Dung it about with enginery of war!" [51]

Crowley did not arrive alone, however. He had brought with him Swiss-born Leah Hirsig, whom he had met in New York while she worked as an elementary school music teacher. They had met through her sister, both of whom were interested in occultism. Crowley and Leah's attraction to each other was immediate and ferocious, and Crowley ultimately consecrated her as his new Scarlet Woman—after several others failed to uphold the task. While he had left the United States without her, his decision to create a communal temple in Cefalu prompted him to send a telegram asking her to join him in Paris, where he had paused in his journey. This she did, pregnant with Crowley's child, and bringing her young son from a previous marriage. Crowley's third child, Anna Leah, affectionately nicknamed "Poupée" after the French word for doll (puppet), was born in Paris in late January 1920.

Crowley then sent Leah and Anna to stay with family in England and arrange some of Crowley's financial matters, as well as to allow for better care of their newborn child. He and their newly acquired nanny, Ninette Shumway, along with her own young son, Howard, moved on to Sicily, where they sought a suitable residence to bring to fruition the ideal Thelemic community. Soon finding a villa to rent near the seashore with the help of the local hotelier, the travel-weary crew settled in and began their work. Leah and Anna joined them in mid-April in the

---

51   Crowley, *The Book of the Law*, 3:4–6.

small complex, flush with funds from a small inheritance Crowley had come into. Crowley himself had set up a temple and consecrated the grounds as the Abbey of Thelema.

Each day at the Abbey would begin with the phrase "Do what thou wilt shall be the whole of the Law!" Meals were prefaced with a saying of *Will*, a form of grace that reaffirmed each participant's investment in the accomplishment of the Great Work. Sex and sex magick were naturally par for the course, as was experimentation with drugs designed to introduce ecstatic states, but equally meditation work along more traditional lines. This location, basking in the Mediterranean sun, brought adherents and aspirants alike to the villa to study with Crowley.

The winds of fortune, good and bad, blew heavily on the Sicilian coast. While the initial summer went well, having the energy and excitement of the villa's conversion to a Thelemic temple at their backs, and several of Crowley's followers joining them over the coming months, conditions at the Abbey began to deteriorate as quickly as the initial inheritance money dwindled. The lush accommodations of the villa ultimately gave way to squalor and sickness given the general lack of sanitary conditions in the small fishing village; but worst of all, Crowley's infant daughter Anna was sick, having arrived from England literally wasting away. The declining conditions at the Abbey could not have helped her recovery. In early October, Leah and the baby went to the nearest hospital for assistance, only to find that it was too late. Crowley was once again devastated by the loss of a young child. A month and a half later, Ninette bore Crowley another child—another girl—Astarte Lulu Panthea.

The British tabloids began to publish sensational articles on the purported debauchery and acts of black magick occurring at the Abbey, and the death of a promising young man from Oxford named Raoul Loveday from typhoid while visiting the Abbey only heightened the furor. While this was no direct cause of the inhabitants, it was unwelcome publicity, and it added insult to the injury of their already tenuous situation: while many of Crowley's supporters sent the occasional donation, it was insufficient means to pay the rent, or even feed them.

Crowley retreated to Paris once again in early 1922, where he had once set off in such high spirits for the foundation of his Abbey of Thelema, now on the brink of collapse. He was also severely addicted to heroin, which was commonly used at the Abbey, and sought to wean himself by magical means from the powerful drug. Bringing his literary talents to bear, he managed to turn the romanticized tale of his addiction and salvation into a pitch for a novel and secured a much-needed advance, resulting in *Diary of a Drug Fiend*. Featuring a romanticized characterization of himself as the spiritual guide of the antagonist, Crowley lays his tale of drug excess, addiction, and eventual recovery against the backdrop of Britain's newly adopted drug laws, which at the time of writing had just been passed. The realism of the novel is of course due to his own experiences, and this ultimately brings the setting back to the Abbey of Thelema as the location of the main characters' cure.

While their misfortunes mounted, it was political interference that ultimately did them in. Mussolini, the same man who had seized power when Crowley was in Rome and was made prime minister of Italy in 1922, ultimately expelled Crowley from the country in late April 1923, though the remaining members were allowed to stay. They carried on for several years after, but the master of the Abbey was now elsewhere, greatly diminishing its intent. Leah's departure from Cefalu, and from The Beast, effectively dissolved the commune in 1927.

Cast to the winds after his expulsion from Italy, Crowley was now forced to live a more or less transient life for the next few years, the relative luxury of his accommodations varying according to the contents of his purse. Nevertheless, he was still focused on advancing Thelema through any means at his disposal, and his dedication never wavered. His fortunes would be blissfully bolstered by a new acquaintance in the guise of Karl Germer, whom he met at a conference in 1925 and who ultimately became Crowley's successor as head of the O.T.O. under the name *Saturnus*. [52]

FURTHER READING

Magick (Book 4)

I Ching

Diary of a Drug Fiend

Little Essays Toward Truth

Late Masterpieces: Thoth and Tears

As the late 1920s gave way to the 1930s, we find Crowley traveling frequently across much of Western Europe and attempting to keep up with a growing O.T.O. presence that he managed to foster in the United States—California, specifically—some of whose leadership had studied with him at the Abbey of Thelema in Cefalu. In the early 1930s, he became deeply enmeshed in the burgeoning art scene in Berlin, being a painter himself endeared to the German expressionists of that time; little came of it financially given the postwar economy and Germany's fabled "reparations," which would ultimately pave the way for a second World War.

Returning to England, he managed to release *The Equinox of the Gods* in 1936, itself a brilliant edition of *The Book of the Law*, replete with the circumstances of its reception and a packet of loose-leaf sheets of the handwritten manuscript reproduced in the back. This handsome edition, coupled with a rededication, sold reasonably well, all things considered, and emboldened Crowley to continue his work in other areas despite boasting a name that had been dragged through the mud by the popular press and the loss of a libel suit in 1935 that strained his already dire financial situation.

---

52   While never stated, it is possible that this name was chosen because the Roman god Saturn "ate his children," an allusion to the formula of sexual magick associated with the O.T.O.!

The one positive note out of his legal misfortunes was that he met Patricia Doherty, who had come to view the trial, sensationalized by the press. Significantly younger than Crowley, Doherty and Crowley became casual acquaintances and thereafter friends. On the heels of yet another failed relationship, and Crowley now sixty years old, he asked her quite out of the blue if she would be willing to bear his child.[53] Perhaps surprisingly, she said yes, and on May 2, 1937, she gave birth to a son, Randall Gair Doherty, though Crowley dubbed him Aleister Ataturk. It was his first boy, and would be his last child.

The 1940s arrived with war on its heels, with Adolf Hitler invading Poland in 1939. The second world war began in earnest, including the blitz on Britain. Though he had retained his contacts in British Intelligence from his days in the first world war, he was in his midsixties and well past the age of any active military service. However, hearing of the occult inclinations of the Third Reich, he did lay claim to the proposition of the "V for Victory!" hand sign that Churchill used throughout the war, allegedly passing it on through his contacts.[54] For Crowley, "V" stood for the destructive power of the Egyptian deity Apophis, leveraged as a counter to the use of the Nazi swastika. If the Nazi high command were as esoterically inclined as was believed, they could not help but understand his intent—or so he surmised.

Crowley had taken up residence at 93 Jermyn Street in London, and despite the constant bombardment throughout the blitz, the wartime rationing, and his ever-precarious health issues, Crowley was active as he could manage in his projects, not least of which was the ambitious *Book of Thoth*, a reimagining of the tarot in the light of his decades of study in alignment with Thelemic philosophy. Detailing each card

---

53 Some accounts have it the other way around, with her asking to bear his child.

54 Crowley had a mutual friend in British Intelligence with author Ian Fleming, of James Bond fame. It is rumored that the original villain in *Casino Royale*, Le Chiffre, was modeled after Crowley!

with intense precision, his vision would be patiently—and sometimes not so patiently—manifested by Lady Frieda Harris, a painter whose style of projective geometry has become the signature style of the deck. The Thoth Tarot deck is imbued with peculiarities not just in its imagery, however. Reverting a change made by Mathers and the Golden Dawn, Crowley returned the Strength card to its original position at number eleven and Justice to its position at eight. Not content to stop there, he then renamed the Justice card "Adjustment" to remove the worldly and subjective concept of justice, which he did not believe to be a natural law. He equally renamed Strength as "Lust" to engender the idea of " ... the joy of strength exercised." [55] In his view, the card intended to show more than mere brutish force, and conceptualize the ecstatic experience of exercising a willed intent. Crowley also renamed Temperance as "Art," noting the subtle balance of forces in the alchemical art depicted therein. The World was also expanded in scope to "the Universe," and Judgment to "the Aeon," which represents a transition from one age to the next rather than the rapturous (or disastrous!) conclusion associated with the Christian Last Judgment.

Most famously, Crowley attempted to solve a problem proposed in *The Book of the Law*: "All these old letters of my Book are aright; but [tzaddi] is not the Star." [56] The eighteenth letter of the Hebrew alphabet, tzaddi, is related to the Star in the tarot by traditional association. Crowley took this statement to imply that the card was misaligned. As a helical pivot on his re-inversion of Strength (Lust) and Justice (Adjustment) cards, he swapped the letters associated with the Emperor and the Star, so that the Star was now attributed to the fifth Hebrew letter, heh, a letter attributed to feminine concepts in traditional Qabalah. This fit the image of the sky goddess Nuit on the card. The Emperor was thereafter associated with tzaddi, where Crowley notes the association with the root term for

---

55   Crowley, *The Book of Thoth*, 92.

56   Crowley, *The Book of the Law*, 1:57.

leaders such a Tsar, Caesar, and so on, with which tzaddi is phonetically sympathetic. The cards retained their positions in the deck, however.

The result was arguably one of the most fascinating tarot decks ever created, a masterpiece integrating Harris's finely executed paintings and Crowley's expertise in detailing the esoteric intricacies of each with the framework of their alchemical roots. A showing of the paintings would also come to pass, with the originals now restored and kept in the War-burg Institute in London.

It was during this time as well that Crowley met a young US Army Captain by the name of Grady Louis McMurtry (1918–1985), who was stationed in Europe during the war and took leave in late 1943 to visit the aging master magician. McMurtry, previously initiated into the O.T.O. while in his home state of California, helped Crowley with some of his publication efforts, but more importantly he eventually became head of the O.T.O. as *Hymenaeus Alpha* in the late sixties, resurrecting the Order from the obscurity into which it had fallen after the death of Crow-ley's immediate successor, Karl Germer, in 1962. McMurtry's work ulti-mately led to the establishment of the O.T.O. as it exists today.

Yet another work came out of Crowley's latter days that sought to capture the knowledge he acquired over his lifetime. A book of magick with essays spanning a broad range of topics, *Aleister Explains Everything* was eventually renamed *Magick Without Tears*, a play on the schoolboy primer *Reading Without Tears*. After all, he thought, why shouldn't everyone be taught the proper fundamentals of magick! The basics of magical rit-ual—pentagrams, hexagrams, circles, and the like—are not to be found here, but instead a litany of essays on aspects of magick and Thelema less touched upon elsewhere.

This book is especially useful to beginners, since it was written through a set of letters between Crowley and an aspirant seeking to learn about magick with little or no background. Thus, we find Crowley being exceptionally lucid about very difficult topics and avoiding the use of terms that might confuse the reader, as so often was the case in his other works, often of necessity.

Even in his introduction, we find the following advice for the beginning student in dedicating themselves to the practice of magick:

1. Perform *Liber Resh vel Helios*.

2. Say *Will* before meals.

3. Keep a Magical Diary.

I equally recommend these practices, which are each further detailed in the later chapters.

FURTHER READING

The Book of Thoth

Magick Without Tears

A Greater Feast

Crowley's final years found him at the Netherwood boarding house in Hastings, England, a city southeast of London on the coast. He arrived in January of 1945, and accounts of his time there note that he had lost none of his wit, and even then introduced himself with the energetic declaration, "Do what thou wilt shall be the whole of the Law." He painted, responded to letters, and visited with friends, old and new alike. He even had one last opportunity to see his young son, who at the time was approaching ten.

One of the individuals he met in his later years at Hastings would come to have as nearly a profound effect on magical practice across the globe as he did: Gerald Gardner (1884–1964), one of the founders of modern witchcraft. Visiting Crowley in 1947, Crowley admitted him into the O.T.O. with the magical motto *Scire,* Latin meaning "To Know." While Gardner never acted on his charter to help reestablish the O.T.O. in England, it was clear that Crowley was a profound influence on him, as many of the rites and rituals of modern witchcraft echo aspects of Crowley's writings and practices. Even the Wiccan Rede is quite familiar, in "An it harm none, *do what thou will,*" among similar variants.[57]

As the summer of 1947 came and went, Crowley's overall health was deteriorating due to both heart and respiratory problems, the latter of which he had suffered throughout his life. (The dangers of smoking were not widely known at the time, though he did have to quit for a time on doctor's orders, to alleviate other conditions.) The oncoming chill of the English winter could not have helped matters, and he furthermore became severely dependent on heroin, used to promote sleep when his asthma otherwise prevented it. Wartime rationing of other medicines forced him to return to the highly addictive drug for a time, and once again, unfortunately, he became addicted.

Aleister Crowley passed away in the late morning of December 1, 1947, at the age of seventy-two, having spent his fortune and his life in support of his art. There are many fantastical stories about his supposed last words, most commonly cited as "I am perplexed," but none of these can be confirmed with any real sense of validity. It is most likely that he passed quietly in his bed, given that he had been confined to it for much of the winter months on doctor's orders.

---

57   Despite often fervent objections, the rede does not predate the modern restoration of witchcraft in the middle half of the twentieth century.

Crowley in his later days at Netherwood, Hastings

His funeral was held four days later in the cold gray weather one might expect of a December 5th in the south of England. Arranged by his good friend Louis Wilkinson, it was a private affair held on public grounds, with readings from Crowley's works, including his *Hymn to Pan* and selections from both *The Book of the Law* and *The Gnostic Mass*.

Of his long friendship with Crowley, Wilkinson recollects, "Some years more will have to pass before this man can be seen as a whole in true perspective. Such a view is always especially hard to take of anyone of whom admiration and vilification have both been carried to extremes. The difficulty is increased in Crowley's case because of the variety and the contradictoriness of the elements in his composition. I do not profess to be able to solve the enigma of his character and his actions. I was glad that he was himself and that I knew him." [58]

Legacy

Crowley's legacy found him fading into relative obscurity apart from a small group of his contemporaries. It was not until the cultural revolution of the 1960s that he began to be recognized for the pioneer that he was. Emerging from the repressive social climate of the United States and elsewhere in the 1950s, the 1960s introduced mainstream society to many of the same things that Crowley was advocating throughout his life: the use of drugs in the pursuit of spiritual awakening, sexual freedom, and (yes) magick, to name but a few.

To give credit where credit is due, the inclusion of Crowley's glowering image on the cover of the Beatles iconic *Sgt. Pepper's Lonely Hearts Club Band* album is most frequently cited as the spark that rekindled interest in the departed magus. Included on the suggestion of John Lennon, Crowley appears second from the left in the top row of historical figures presented behind the band.

---

58 Louis Wilkinson, *Seven Friends*, 63.

Given the popularity of the Beatles at the time, and the ground-breaking album that it was, fans naturally wanted to know everything about the people adorning the cover—and there was Aleister Crowley, the countercultural icon in waiting.

Crowley's depiction as the "evil" magician and early rock-and-roll's fascination with the occult, born of its musical roots in American blues and that genre's own relationship with tales of the devil, equally advanced the mythos of Crowley after his death. Perhaps no greater association can be found than Led Zeppelin guitarist Jimmy Page, who was a fan of Crowley and brought his life and work into the cultural spotlight as well. Many magical elements were included in Page's "dream sequence" in their concert film *The Song Remains the Same*, and the signature phrase "Do what thou wilt" was inscribed in the wax of some pressings of their third album. Page purchased Crowley's Boleskine estate in 1970, though it appears he rarely spent time there. He is reported to have collected a number of Crowley's works. Other musicians have picked up on this current as well, including David Bowie, who had a keen interest in occultism in general, and the Golden Dawn and Crowley in particular. Ozzy Osbourne released the song *Mr. Crowley* in 1980, continuing a musical fascination with the "wickedest man in the world."

The influence of Crowley is no longer relegated to counterculture references, however. A 2002 poll by the BBC of the hundred greatest Britons listed none other than Crowley among its ranks, at a respectable number seventy-three. Aside from his own autohagiography, several scholars in recent years have picked up the mantle of producing a compelling biography, not least among which are *Perdurabo: The Life of Aleister Crowley* by Richard Kaczynski, *Aleister Crowley: The Biography* by Tobias Churton, and *Do What Thou Wilt: A Life of Aleister Crowley* by Lawrence Sutin. I highly recommend any or all of them for a greater understanding of his life.

Crowley is just now beginning to have his day in the sun.

2

Philosophy

Given the historical reference to Crowley's life, brief as that small biography might be, we have a means of understanding how Crowley "the man" became Crowley "the prophet of a new aeon." Wait—what? Prophet? Well... why not?

Crowley's unique life, background, and experience placed him in a position to receive, accept, and ultimately promulgate Thelema, the pursuit of which became the focus of his whole life. He was also a prolific writer with an exceptional command of the English language, and that talent allowed him to communicate the often-difficult sentiments of such an abstract philosophy in his writings. It is from these writings, both published and personal, that we can seek our answers about the intent of Thelema and how it applies to ourselves.

I must also provide a standard disclaimer that any statements made in this work indicate either direct quotations from Crowley or my own present beliefs and experiences, and I will try my best to ensure I separate the two. The only true authority died with Crowley himself—excepting *you* of course. That's right. As we will see, in Thelema, every individual is responsible for determining—and reevaluating—their own set of beliefs through their own experience, and should your beliefs at some point come to disagree with what is presented here, then that's just perfectly fine. In fact, I would encourage it!

The Philosophy of Thelema

"The word of the law is Θέλημα."

—*Liber AL vel Legis* (*The Book of the Law*)

The spiritual and social philosophy that Crowley spent his life defining and manifesting is known as Thelema. *Thelema* means "will" in Greek, spelled Qelhma, and adherents to the philosophy are generally known as *Thelemites*. Based on his acceptance and understanding of *The Book of the Law*, Crowley holds Thelema apart from many religious movements in that it is highly individualistic and focuses on every individual *doing their will*. There is no universal moral that every adherent must be held accountable to, save for that one injunction, whose exercise and practice is left to every individual.

Do What Thou Wilt

Perhaps the best-known (and equally misunderstood) tenet of Thelema is held in its principal maxim: *Do what thou wilt shall be the whole of the Law.* It is without a doubt the most potent expression of the central idea of Thelema, and without context seems to advocate the abandonment of all principled behavior entirely! However, doing your *will* is quite different than doing what you *want*, and considerably more difficult. After all, the hedonistic acquiescence to every fleeting whim is likely a distraction from what you feel you should be doing with your life. Though momentarily fulfilling, staying true to your will requires a great deal more discipline than most people think. What you *will* to do is truly your life's calling, discovered over time as the natural course of an introspective life steers you toward an understanding of who you are.

Love Is the Law

The second component to this maxim is "Love is the law, love under will."
By division, we cause hatred and dis-ease: love is that which unites. The
phrase alludes to a fundamental concept in Thelema, which is that the ideas
of "good" and "bad" are not universal. They are entirely subjective experiences and are generally qualified based on the social and religious climate of
the time, rather than your own innate understanding. The phrase appears
in the fifty-seventh verse of the first chapter of *The Book of the Law*, and Crowley's own commentary on that passage redirects the reader to several chapters
in another of his works, *Liber Aleph: The Book of Wisdom or Folly*. [59] Each of these
chapters focuses on this specific ideal: that even those things by which you
are repulsed can be overcome by love.

This latter statement deserves some attention. We are likely familiar
with what this sort of sentiment means in our general society today, and
it is decidedly *not* what we intend it to mean in Thelema. Nearly everyone
sees "love" as the way of their religion, but the expression of that love is
too often falsely borne of the ego: they expect the way of love to be a "poor
sinner coming to the recognition of their faults." It is arrogant, in that
they presume their moral stance is superior, when in fact it is entirely
arbitrary. Thelema posits that each and every person should develop their
own moral code, and *through love* they can come to understand the need and
virtue of all things that are part of the universe. Crowley notes that when
Lao Tzu was questioned where the Tao was, he referred the enquirer to a
pile of dung; the Buddha noted that there was no grain of dust that would
not reach enlightenment in and through its own way.

Individuation

As a child, born completely free of any external psychological influences
or pressures, you are as much "you" as you may ever be. As you grow

---

59 "Aleph" is the first letter of the Hebrew alphabet and in the Western magical
    tradition related to the Fool card of the tarot, who in turn represents both folly
    outwardly and sublime spiritual enlightenment inwardly.

older, you are exposed to certain expectations about behavior, dress, and similar conformities that need to be followed to conform to and function in the society in which you are entrenched. Failing to observe these customs is likely to bring mockery, scorn, and even overt punishment. These social, religious, and familial pressures, while often well intentioned, essentially warp, bury, or pervert your concept of your essential "you-ness." This was extremely important from an evolutionary perspective when the capacity to select your social group was limited and the price of expulsion from that group was likely death.

However, after tens of thousands of years of biological evolution to reinforce this idea, we have made exceptional strides in social evolution over perhaps the last few thousand, accelerating greatly with the technologies of the last few hundred. We have large cities and massive populations from which we can actually *pick* our social groups, generally, as well as our religious influences, if any. Family, as they say, you're stuck with—but is that even really true? It is difficult, but it certainly doesn't bear the risk of death it once did if an individual decides to sever those relationships. Do note that I am not *advocating* this dissociation in any sense, only illustrating the vast scope of social evolution that has occurred over a very short amount of time.

Equally, it is easy for us to say, "Well, I'm not part of the herd," but science says otherwise, and a complete withdrawal from the social fabric is usually indicative of a rather severe mental disorder. What we are really saying when we echo this sentiment is that we have *found a better herd*, one that speaks more directly to our own innate understanding of who we are and what we want to be—or at least one that opposes what we don't. In Thelema, you are urged to define your own ideals and moral code, which may indeed lead you away from the confines of the social circles that you have identified with to that point—but isn't that what prompted you to begin searching in the first place?

Thelema represents a view of the world that truly began to take root in the philosophers of the nineteenth century as scientific progress (and arguably an equal spiritual regression) swept across the cultural landscape, where now each individual is not just able to define who they are, they are somewhat *obligated* to do so. In the modern age, at least in more established societies, conformity to a specific social order is less important than it once was, largely because there is such a multiplicity. Yet, the religions of the old age still natter on about their competing versions of conformity according to the will of their particular board of directors.

With this freedom (and responsibility) must also come the acceptance of another's capacity to do likewise. It does us no good to walk around asserting our right to do something and ignore that effective right in every other person. That's just being a bully: it's not likely to end well, and it's certainly not going to bring you any closer to an understanding of *your will* since that sort of negative behavior is solely about what you *want*. So, consider that the phrase "Do what thou wilt" might speak not to yourself but to the person you are speaking to, thereby recognizing their autonomy as well as your own. I think that idea is important to keep in mind, because as Thelemites the idea of asserting another's right is as important as asserting our own.

FURTHER READING
Liber Aleph: The Book of Wisdom or Folly
Little Essays Toward Truth

The Religion of Thelema

You may be asking, "Is Thelema a new religion?" It is a fair question, and Crowley addresses this topic directly in his book *Magick Without Tears* under a chapter bearing exactly that title. In it he notes that Thelema *is* a religion in as much as it adheres to the standard definition: a set of beliefs, hopefully with reasonable internal consistency. However, it is important to note that he has definite reservations about the term "religion," specifically, saying, "Call it a new religion, then, if it so please [you]; but I confess that I fail to see what you have gained by so doing, and I feel bound to add that you might easily cause a great deal of misunderstanding, and work a rather stupid kind of mischief. The word does not occur in *The Book of the Law*." [60]

Does he contradict himself in saying that Thelema is *not* a religion? No! Rather, he alludes to the fact that many people have a preconceived notion of what religion is, tainted by their own negative or positive experiences, that will inevitably be "brought along" into their understanding of Thelema—a "stupid kind of mischief" that will hamper their capacity to understand Thelema as anything but a *replacement* for the set of moral codes they are seeking to abandon, as well as dragging along all of the baggage that they have associated with the term.

One can certainly state that it is a religion in the sense of upholding a spiritual philosophy—in harmony with scientific method and observation, of course. Many Thelemites consider it a religion, as evidenced by the Thelemic basis of the Gnostic Mass of *Ecclesia Gnostica Catholica*, or Gnostic Catholic Church, while others simply believe it to be a spiritual philosophy that need not encumber itself with the idea of religion. So, if you are uncomfortable with calling it a religion, then call it a philosophy, and vice versa—just be honest with yourself about why you are inclined to do one or the other.

As a *new religious movement*, it resembles many others in being syncretic—a collection of ideas, iconography, and themes adapted from earlier religious contexts, specifically in the representation of the Egyptian gods and the liturgical context of the Gnostic Mass, to name but a few. However, its obvious differentiator is that it does not stem from a different (or even radical) interpretation of a preexistent text, but rather from the original dispensation that is *The Book of the Law*.

---

60   Crowley, *Magick Without Tears*, 219.

Do Thelemites Worship?

If we look at Thelema as a religion, it is fair to ask whether that religion has one or more deities and if they are worshipped by its adherents. From even a cursory glance at *The Book of the Law*, its central text, the Thelemic trinity of Nuit, Hadit, and Ra-Hoor-Khuit stands out as a reasonably strong suggestion that Thelema is in fact a deistic religion. However, under the surface, it is not quite that simple.

When we use the term "worship," it implies a sense of reverence or awe, typically reserved for or conveyed toward a deity. The word occurs eleven times in *The Book of the Law*, with variants (worshipped, etc.) occurring five more times. Relevant passages include:

- In chapter **one**, we are admonished to "Worship the Khabs ... ," [61] where Khabs is interpreted as the Inner Light or sole Truth of the individual.

- In chapter **two**, we are—somewhat conversely—urged to not worship Hadit, for it is Hadit who is the worshipper and drawn unto Nuit, the infinite.

- In chapter **three**, we are told to convey the Stele of Revealing as an object of worship, as well as to worship the warlike Ra-Hoor-Khuit with fire, blood, and steel, setting his image in the East and clustering around him like images to support him. [62]

It is in the third and final chapter that we find references to worship as we might typically define it, and the Stele of Revealing is set in the east at the top of the super-altar in the Gnostic Mass, the central rite of the O.T.O., a ceremony of religious expression along Thelemic lines. However, even considering the liturgical rite that is the Gnostic Mass, the congregants there are not *worshipping* in the sense of directing praise at the principal deities. They are present to partake in the Eucharistic

---

61   Crowley, *Libel AL vel Legis*, I:9.

62   In this latter passage, Crowley is instructed that he would obtain a specific image of Ra-Hoor-Khuit that would serve as the primary focus.

rite of the mass, and in so doing express a sense of awe and reverence toward the source of all life (as represented by the sun and "the Lord"), which does in a sense meet the criteria of worship as defined above. Though others may disagree, it is reasonable to suggest that the Gnostic Mass does in fact qualify as a ceremony of worship toward the principles aforementioned, though the term likely suffers from the same sort of "mischief" in bringing along one's own preconceptions, which Crowley notes with respect to religion in general. So, as with so many aspects of Thelema, the answer is: it's complicated.

Aside from the Gnostic Mass, many Thelemites do pay tribute to or otherwise "worship" deities from cultural pantheons outside of Thelema, such as those from Hindu cultures (Ganesha, etc.), Afro-Caribbean practices (Loas, Orishas, etc.), and similar devotional traditions—almost as a form of folk magick. In so doing, they tend to reserve Thelemic deities and practices for greater spiritual matters, while the extra-Thelemic icons are generally more for common household magick. In no sense do Thelemites consider those deities Thelemic in intent or origin, or even part of the general corpus of beliefs, but Thelema as a religion does not generally frown on drawing in practices from non-Western religions, likely because of Crowley's own religious appropriations and admixtures—vis-à-vis Frazer's *The Golden Bough*. Given that much of Thelema is in principle drawn against the major religions of the last few thousand years, however, there is some leeway in interpretation when bringing these deities into practice: in short, they often bring the god but not the doctrine. It is difficult to reconcile Judeo-Christian religious practices with Thelema, for obvious reasons, though even these are commonly leveraged within the scope of magical practices that originate in those religious contexts. These occur in the practices associated with Solomonic or Western ceremonial magick in general, which is a common interest among Thelemites due to Crowley's own focus on them during various phases of his life, especially during his time in the Golden Dawn.

The Stele of Revealing

A principal focal point for Thelemic imagery is the Stele of Revealing, which is placed at the apex of the super-altar in the temple for the Gnostic Mass. This is the same funerary stele that Rose indicated in the Boulak Museum as containing the "proper" image of Horus as Ra-Hoor-Khuit, the one that Crowley was distinctly instructed to obtain a copy of during the reception of *The Book of the Law*. It is the funerary stele of the priest Ankh-af-na-Khonsu, and contains Nuit as the dark, feminine figure arching over the top, Hadit as the winged solar disk thereunder, and Ra-Hoor-Khuit receiving an offering from Ankh-af-na-Khonsu himself.

The Stele of Revealing (front and back)

Crowley originally had the stele translated from the hieroglyphics into French by the assistant to the curator of the museum. From there, he versified the stele into more poetic form, with due poetic license from the actual translation. The first stanza is given as:

Above, the gemmed azure is
The naked splendour of Nuit;
She bends in ecstasy to kiss
The secret ardours of Hadit.
The winged globe, the starry blue
Are mine, O Ankh-f-n-Khonsu. [63]

It is important to note that the term *Stele of Revealing* for this funeral stele is only common parlance to Thelemites.

Sin

It would be remiss of me to avoid discussing the concept of "sin" in Thelema, as inseparable as it is with the concept of religion itself. After all, what's religion without the idea of transgression? Bluntly, "a whole lot better." If the will and morality of an individual is determined for everyone, each for themselves, then is there no such concept as sin? What would stop someone from simply going out and murdering people in line at the local coffee shop simply to get a jump start on their latte? Addressing this is yet another well-known and equally misunderstood phrase in *The Book of the Law*, "The word of sin is Restriction." [64]

The Book of the Law notes that "Every man and every woman is a star." [65] Crowley expounds on this idea by stating that every individual must have their own path through the cosmos. This path is our True Will, in harmony with the Universal Will of the cosmos, and if we simply let that

---

63   Crowley, *The Equinox of the Gods*, 1:14

64   Crowley, *The Book of the Law*, I:41.

65   Ibid., I:3.

course direct us, then we will be all the happier for it. The trouble comes when we are distracted from that course: we feel the strain of gravitation to our true path, and worse yet we start bumping into things that may or may not be in the groove of their own respective orbits. This is an allegory for interpersonal conflict, and by its resolution demonstrates the idea that if we are all doing our True Will, then there will not be conflict.

This is perhaps overly fanciful, but "No religion has failed hitherto by not promising enough…"[66] These, again, are allegories that point the way: if you are sticking to your own path, then the wanderings of other stars are less of a concern to you—even should they bump into you! The strength of your course will overcome and you will move on.

When we think of sin in the Judeo-Christian context, it is either inherited from the misdeeds of our forefathers or a personal failure to uphold the interpretations of the observed *legal* injunctions of the relevant holy book. Each category generally represents a failure in the direction of excess, be it pride, gluttony, covetousness, and so on. In Thelema, we can recognize that these outwardly excessive actions are manifestations of inward restriction—a lashing out against the confines of a social and religious fabric that has caused them to deviate from the path of their True Will. The more they wander off route, the more difficult it can be to find the way back, and the more terribly their psyche reacts.

Evil (So Called) and Black Magick

With Crowley's amusing reputation as "the wickedest man in the world," his self-identification with "The Beast" of the Christian apocalypse, and his ideas on the nature of sin from a religious context, it stands to reason that he might have a somewhat different point of view from his contemporaries when it comes to the philosophical problem of evil—which is to say, his *Christian* contemporaries. That Thelema might vary from the view held by the prevailing religious doctrines should come as no surprise,

---

66 Crowley, *Magick*, 7.

but how does Thelema treat a core theological issue that lies at the root of nearly every religious philosophy?

The view of Thelema is simple: evil itself is a subjective human construct. Think about this idea for a moment. What are its ramifications? Well, first you have to acknowledge that varying cultures and religions have very different views of evil, and therefore right and wrong, justice, et cetera. This can be readily observed even within the scope of a *single* culture and religion, whose ideas and opinions may vary both with locality and time. "[Justice] has none but a purely human and therefore relative sense; so it is not to be considered as one of the facts of Nature." [67] Thelema cannot assert a concept of good and evil, as there is no universal moral on which to hang that hat.

That having been said, I am sure your mind is now racing across all of the most horrific acts ever imagined by god or man. Surely those must qualify as evil, even in Thelema. To this I can say only two things. The first is that *nature does not care*. At an infinite scope, pulling away in perspective from our current location, to the planet, solar system, galaxy, galactic cluster, and ultimately the vast and barren expanse of the known and unknown universe, even the worst calamity imaginable on our nigh-imperceptible speck of rock seems reasonably insignificant. Were the planet to be wiped out entirely, we might at best scatter our debris somewhat inconveniently at an indifferent Mars. Secondly, a universal consensus of subjective belief does not make something objectively true. If everyone in the room, or on the planet for that matter, believed you could fly, including yourself, your defenestration would still end poorly—subjectively, of course.

> Until the Great work has been performed, it is presumptuous for the Magician to pretend to understand the universe, and dictate its policy. Only the Master of the Temple can say

---

67   Crowley, *The Book of Thoth*, 86.

whether any given act is a crime. "Slay that innocent child?" (I hear the ignorant say.) "What a horror!" "Ah!" replies the Knower, with foresight of history, "but that child will become Nero. Hasten to strangle him!" There is a third, above these, who understands that Nero was as necessary as Julius Caesar.[68]

That being said, Crowley made some definitive statements about the concept of black magick, which falls somewhat under the purview of evil. Oft accused of being a black magician himself, he took pains to define what black magick was within the scope of his philosophy. In *Magick*, he notes, "But 'to sell one's soul to the devil,' to renounce no matter what for an equivalent in personal gain, is black magick. You are no longer a noble giver of your all, but a mean huckster."[69] He also classifies any force of magick for material ends as inherently black magick, including in this lot "Christian Scientists, Mental Healers, Professional Diviners, Psychics, and the like."[70] It's not necessarily that these practices are in and of themselves wrong, but that their practice *for money* is against the idea of giving yourself over to the betterment of the universe. It is a misappropriation. To this end, his magical Order of the A∴ A∴ still prohibits the taking of money for magical teaching or effects of any kind, under penalty of expulsion.

To trade away the powers of the universe with which you have been bestowed for material gain is one aspect in his definition of black magick, but there is an even more consistent thread through his writing: the concept of *imbalance*. In writing on black magick in *Magick*, Crowley notes that the principal aim of any aspirant is to raise themselves "in a vertical straight line."[71] He follows this statement with the idea that any

---

68 Crowley, *Magick*, 275.
69 Ibid., 169.
70 Ibid., 276.
71 Ibid., 275.

deviation from this line either tends *toward* or *is* black magick. I find that this concept is demonstrated most ably in *The Book of Thoth*, with Crowley's modification and description of the Justice card, traditionally shown as a woman holding scales and a sword. He renamed Justice as Adjustment and presented it with similar imagery. As justice is not something observed in nature, he chose to define this card as adjustment, with the idea of reestablishing an equilibrium as the definition of a natural and therefore "good" state. He comments thereafter that "Equilibrium stands apart from any individual prejudices ... "[72]

Imbalance creates stress within the universe—your universe. This is ably demonstrated in the physical world by standing up and leaning to one side. Compared to standing absolutely vertical, it places an additional burden on the muscles, causing strain. The more imbalance you create, the more stress it takes to keep reasonably upright—until the point where the muscles give or gravity takes over and you tumble to the floor. This is true in all things: physically, emotionally, intellectually, and spiritually. Thus, it is a principal duty of each magician—and we are *all* magicians—to seek their own equilibrium on all planes.

Death

Death and how it is perceived is a central concept in most, if not all, religions, with views of the afterlife ranging broadly from perpetual bliss to eternal torment—or perhaps just a calm dissolution into *the void*. So, how does Thelema view the idea? As you might suspect, it's quite a bit better than eternal damnation. Contrary to many religious viewpoints, Thelema views death *as a completely natural occurrence that should therefore be free of fear*. Death, in fact, should be celebrated as an inevitable step in the natural order of things and a necessary consequence of your incarnation, despite the fact that those of us left behind will generally miss the deceased individual and the patterns they have made in our daily lives.

---

72   Crowley, *The Book of Thoth*, 87.

As Crowley's own father often preached, " ... and then?" What about
the afterlife? Crowley did appear to believe in reincarnation through
much of his adult life, or at least the possibility of it, though that fact
by no means implies that you must believe the same in order to be considered a Thelemite. [73] There is no equivalent Heaven, and certainly no
equivalent Hell, with his reincarnationist philosophies deriving from
his early exposure to and satisfaction in the tenets of Buddhism. However, his Gnostic Mass captures the Thelemic concept of death and the
afterlife in the tenth and eleventh Collects, where the congregants stand
with their eyes open and heads erect:

> Term of all that liveth, whose name is inscrutable, be favour-
> able to us in thine hour. Unto them from whose eyes the veil
> of life hath fallen may there be granted the accomplishment of
> their true Wills; whether they will absorption in the Infinite,
> or to be united with their chosen and preferred, or to be in
> contemplation, or to be at peace, or to achieve the labour and
> heroism of incarnation on this planet or another, or in any
> Star, or aught else, unto them may there be granted the accom-
> plishment of their wills; yea, the accomplishment of their wills.
> **AUMGN. AUMGN. AUMGN.**

Thus, in the final observances of the Collects, eleven short orations
on the principles of the Gnostic Mass, we find a broad spectrum of possible outcomes and perceptions of the afterlife, each affirming the will of
the congregant in its own way. So, as far as I am concerned, you are free
to believe what you like, but we have most certainly cast aside the super-
stitions of the past in affirming the natural course of events that is death.

---

73   For example, the present author does not believe in an afterlife, but asserts the
right of every individual to decide for themselves. It won't matter to him: he'll
be dead!

The Great Work

"The Single Supreme Ritual is the attainment of the Knowledge and Conversation of the Holy Guardian Angel. It is the raising of the complete man in a vertical straight line. Any deviation from this line tends to become black magic. Any other operation is black magick."

—*Magick*, Chapter XXI

As previously indicated, and in a marked departure from the strictures of older religions, Thelema asserts the capacity to develop and define your own moral code rather than adhering to a set of universal principles that are ultimately arbitrary and overly simplistic. Its ethos hinges on personal freedom, accountability, and no small amount of introspection. The difficulty in attaining this ideal is twofold: firstly to determine through careful consideration and experience what that code is, and secondly to hold yourself accountable to that code. The process of determining the first, and doing the latter, is known as the Great Work.

This accomplishment, also referred to as the "Knowledge and Conversation of your Holy Guardian Angel," contacting your "Divine Genius," or any number of similar epithets related to spiritual attainment you are likely to hear passed around, is a core principle of Thelema. This idea far predated Crowley, but he specifically chose to refer to this process or path of attainment as the obtaining of the Knowledge and Conversation of the Holy Guardian Angel, because "The theory implied in these words is so patently absurd that only simpletons would waste much time in analyzing it." [74] In short, he purposely selected the most intellectually meaningless title in order to emphasize that the process itself was not one of intellectual pursuit. Therein lies a very meaningful comment to the nature of the Great Work: while you may study intensely to find the path, the path itself is not one of intellectual pursuit but self-discovery.

---

74   Crowley, *Magick*, 153.

Oft considered the hallmark of the magical adept, all these terms fall absurdly short of describing exactly what the Great Work is and means to the individual. In fact, it is more common to define these ideas in the negative: it is "not" something—it is unfathomable, inexplicable, ineffable, and so on. In that vein, let me make a statement about the Great Work: the Great Work is not something that *other* people do; it is something *you* do.

The Great Work is not only a central theme of Thelema, but the central theme of your whole life. It is yours to set out and *do*. So, what is it? What does that mean? In short, the Great Work is the process of finding out precisely who you are and what you want to do with your life—then doing it. The above-mentioned process of discovering your own moral code is in fact the process of discovering who you truly are as a person. Your sense of morality then comes about as a natural by-product of that understanding. You don't actually start out by attempting to define your own moral compass, but by working to discover who you truly are—a center of consciousness in the universe of all potential experience. Your own sense of self-direction when unencumbered by external expectations, the undeterred arc of your star through the infinite, is known as your True Will.

Fortunately, there is a means of determining your True Will, and that method is something with which Crowley is inexorably connected: magick.

Magick

You may have noticed, here and elsewhere, the archaic spelling of *magick*, adding the final "k" to the more common "magic." Crowley instituted this practice to distinguish the art from stage magic or legerdemain, which are simply parlor tricks designed for amusement. While there are other methods of mystical and magical attainment, including the practice of raja yoga that Crowley integrated into his own practices, I believe that the true purpose of magick is to discover your own potential, power, and place in the world: your True Will. It is all too common that practitioners of magick both ancient and modern promise spectacular powers, often supernatural in scope, to the prospective student of the art, but let me nip this in the bud immediately: *Magick can give you no powers of which you were not capable in the first place, nor any powers beyond the scope of nature itself.*

To address this in no uncertain terms, Crowley defined magick in his work of the same name as follows:

MAGICK
is the Science and Art
of causing Change
to occur in conformity with Will[75]

So far, so good! So, you ask, if I just will something to occur, I can make it happen? To a degree, yes. The first caveat to this is that you have to truly *will* it, not just *want* or *wish* it to happen. The latter two words imply a sense of idleness or passivity; will is action. For example, I can want an ice cream all I like, but that desire is not going to manifest until I arrive at the window of an ice cream shop with the financial means to purchase it at a time when they are selling it. Alternately, you could sit outside that same shop and meditate strongly on wanting an ice cream until someone asks what the hell you're doing and, amused at your behavior, decides to buy you that same ice cream on a whim, but it's less certain and a bit of a con.

The second principle is the one far too many people miss, despite given immediately after Crowley's famous definition of magick:

Any required Change
may be effected by the application
of the proper kind and degree of force
in the proper manner
through the proper medium
to the proper object.[76]

75   Crowley; *Magick*, 128.
76   Crowley, *Magick*, 128.

This statement is less direct, but it essentially implies that you must act through the proper channels in order to obtain your result. Let's return to our example. We must apply the proper kind and degree of force (currency) in the proper manner (at a time and place when the shop is open) through the proper medium (the store) to the proper object (a person working at the store). If we attempt to give them money from another country, representing the wrong kind of force, we may be less capable of obtaining our end. Similarly, if we attempt to give our money to the wrong person, such as someone else in line, we are not acting through the proper medium on the proper object. They can't help us with our ice cream problem, but they might well be capable of helping us out of our money, which simply compounds our problem!

There is a further implication in that statement, however: you have to be capable of *providing* the proper kind and degree of force. I can do a great number of things, but I can't control the weather, shoot fire from my eyes (or more amusing parts of my body), bench press a car, or turn water into wine. The same, I am sad to say, goes for you. Nature reigns supreme, and you must still work within her laws.

Now, let's further refine our definition and purpose:

> **Magick is the Science of understanding oneself**
> **And one's conditions.**
> **It is the Art of applying that understanding in action.** [77]

All of the practices that will be given in the latter section of this book are magical in their own right, but each has a specific purpose, even if it is not readily evident: to bring you to a better understanding of yourself and your ability to effect real change in the world around you. In fact, in order to effect the greatest change, you must first come to an understanding of who you are.

---

77   Ibid.

Otherwise your conscious thoughts and actions may be in conflict with, and subverted by, your actual desire: your True Will. "For pure will, unassuaged of purpose, delivered from the lust of result, is in every way perfect." [78] This is at the root of all neurosis, and people at war with themselves cannot hope to achieve much of value until that conflict is resolved. Worse yet, their greatest gains are likely to be those that most counter their True Will, as the conscious mind fights the subconscious with increasing vigor!

On that note, an understanding of yourself is completely undermined by both the *illusion* of having power that you do not have and the *disillusionment* of coming to that same conclusion. Avoid each of these pitfalls by returning always to a position of skepticism. This term does not mean doubt: once begun, you must never doubt! The word itself comes from the idea of *questioning*, despite its use in common language, implying a neutral, unbiased position. Consider first whether you truly will something to manifest, then also whether it is something in your power to manifest, then how you may manifest it. Then, if each of these is in place and proper, *act* without reservation, hindrance, or doubt. Crowley included on the frontispiece of *The Equinox, Volume 1*, the phrase, "The Method of Science. The Aim of Religion" in deference to this idea: everything you do through magical practice must be rigorously tested in its efficacy so that chance conditions do not convince you of powers you do not have and positive successes can be enhanced by further experiment.

Be honest with yourself.

Know Thy Self.

---

78 Crowley, *The Book of the Law*, I:44.

The Magick of Abramelin

"My adepts stand upright; their head above the heavens, their feet below the hells."

—Liber Tzaddi vel Hamus Hermeticus [79]

A treatise that Crowley considered of the utmost importance, *The Sacred Magic of Abramelin the Mage* is a well-known ceremonial text, largely devotional in nature and inexorably connected to the idea of the Great Work. Written in the fifteenth century, it tells the tale of a man traveling the world seeking enlightenment, in vain, until he is finally brought to a master by the name of Abramelin, who instructs him on how to attain the Knowledge and Conversation of his Holy Guardian Angel through constant prayer and devotion. S. L. MacGregor Mathers, head of the Golden Dawn and mentor to Crowley, provided an English translation from a manuscript found in the Parisian *Bibliothèque de l'Arsenal*, though Crowley notes having been directed to the work as early as 1898. [80] He purchased his Scottish highland home, Boleskine, specifically to undertake the work there.

There are a number of conditions regarding both the operation and the operator that are noted in the book, including gender (male, of course), age, parentage, and so on—all aspects that the modern practitioner can safely disregard as thoroughly outdated cultural bigotries of the time. However, other aspects are curiously tolerant, such as noting the individual should undertake the operation under the beliefs of their present religion: there is no attempt at conversion. Other magical opinions are given so as to provide the reader with a particular point of view when it comes to undertaking this monumental task, such as the time of day, the arrangement of the temple in which to perform the operation, and similar

---

79   Crowley, "Liber Tzaddi," *The Holy Books of Thelema*, v. 40

80   Crowley, *The Equinox of the Gods*, 54.

accouterments relevant to a magical operation, each of which can be left to the judgment of the practitioner performing the work.

While the translation that Crowley read describes a six-month operation of three two-month periods, modern translations show that there are actually three six-month periods, making the operation significantly longer in duration. [81] However, since many initiates have undertaken the operation successfully using the former, incorrect translation of Mathers's French manuscript, it is once more the prerogative of the practitioner to determine the appropriate time span. What is certain is that the operation should begin on or around the spring equinox and end on or around the fall equinox.

The first period begins with daily orations or prayers, but with relatively little other incursion into the daily life of the individual. The second and third periods intensify both the duration of the prayers and withdrawal from daily life until such time as the adherent invokes his or her Holy Guardian Angel—often abbreviated simply as HGA. This invocation releases a significant force in the magician, and they are compelled by the book to call forth a host of infernal spirits in order to compel them into submission by the might and authority of their angel. It also permits the magician to unlock the secrets of a number of magical squares for the purposes of generally beneficial (but ultimately mundane) aims. Thus, much like many similar treatises, there is a focus on a highly spiritual attainment that provides a means to a very tangible end, and the so-called "Abramelin Squares" were venerated (if not feared) by members of the Golden Dawn for their potency. Even so, this can be seen as one of the many "spiritual gifts" that are available to the magician, but in many cases this continual use blocks further advancement: for after the Abramelin Operation, the Holy Guardian Angel becomes the sole spiritual authority over the individual, who can then seek out their true will and self-identity through the relationship with that intermediary.

---

81   Dehn and Guth, *The Book of Abramelin*, xvii.

This, far above and beyond any tangible benefits, is the primary purpose of pursuing the arduous path that is the Operation.

FURTHER READING

The Book of Abramelin (Denn & Guth)

The Book of the Sacred Magic of Abramelin the Mage (Mathers)

Into the Abyss

If I were to tell you that the end-goal of the Great Work was to face the dreadful demon Choronzon, pour every ounce of your blood into the Cup of Babalon, annihilating your Self and becoming a Babe of the Abyss, it is reasonably safe to presume that this book would close with a sudden and permanent clap of its pages. Well...

The concept of the Abyss is a difficult one, but it is one inherent to Thelema, and despite the rather difficult apocalyptic symbolism used to describe it, it represents a very advanced stage of spiritual development—and one that most never attain. To understand this phase of initiation, we must look back once more at the Holy Guardian Angel, what it represents, and the path forward from that revelation.

The attainment of the Holy Guardian Angel, from a psychological perspective, is a manifest personification of your subconscious self, and thereby becomes the "spiritual teacher" that you have always truly longed for. (There is an old saying that if you are seeking a spiritual teacher, then just begin your journey without, and a teacher will present themselves—that teacher is an allusion to the HGA.) So, you have a guide to commune with your inner Self, but that leaves you still one degree of separation apart from your *True Self*. It's significantly better than having no compass whatsoever, and a tremendous experience, but now what?

It takes a significant amount of self-work to attain the HGA, balancing and introspecting the four elements of your psyche: earth, air, water, and fire—body, intellect, emotion, and aspiration, respectively. With the attainment of the HGA, you have broken through a barrier where you can begin to understand who you truly are and formulate your own sense of self, bit by bit. Conversely, this means *breaking down* the prior constructs of who you thought you were previously. While the initial phase of initiation is anabolic, or upbuilding, the second phase is catabolic, or a tearing down. You must peel away the layers of the ego—self and the persona that others, including yourself, have created around and about you.

True to form, Crowley wraps a lot of this process in the same apocalyptic imagery as his beastly moniker, but what the Abyss is truly about is the dissolution of the ego, and even the most peaceful of Buddhists can smile in accordance with that! If the HGA represents a window to the self, then "crossing the Abyss" ultimately represents walking in the front door and making yourself at home. The reason that it is so difficult is that you must tear down your ego and become what Crowley calls a Babe of the Abyss, reducing your ego to nothing, just as it was when you were born. The guardian of this Abyss, to whom Crowley refers as Choronzon,[82] is the ego itself, ceaselessly distracting and perverting your identity from its source of truth: "Bodily functions are part of the machine; silent, unless in dis-ease. But mind, never at ease, creaketh 'I'." [83] So, it's not so much as making yourself at home: it's more like tearing down the old house you'd been cramped into and building the home you had in mind in the first place.

Crowley notes the Oath of the Abyss as, 'I swear to interpret every phenomenon as a particular dealing of God with my Soul,' [84] which of course is a first-class ticket to madness (and self-delusion) unless you're at a particular initiatory stage to understand it in its proper context—and let's be clear that this is after years and years of intense spiritual work. In

---

82   According to Crowley, Choronzon was taken from the tenth of thirty "aethyrs" of the Enochian system of magick created (or received) by Dr. John Dee in the latter part of the sixteenth century, that aethyr corresponding to the self-same spiritual experience.

83   Crowley, "Steeped Horsehair," *The Book of Lies*, ch. 8.

84   Crowley, *Magick*, 182.

order to be successful in this aim, we must be willing to give what we perceive to be our own self over, completely silencing the ego-self. Hence, we find the image of the Cup of Babalon, the Universal Mother, and the idea of giving every ounce of your blood/life/self unto it, the universal life. To the preexistent ego, it feels like a sacrifice, but in reality it is a stripping away of all those parts of you that were not *truly you*.

Simple, right? The trouble is that the ego that you are trying to destroy is the very ego observing itself being propelled toward its own demise, and if there is one thing the ego hates, it is the idea of its own end. Thus, it often occurs that on the precipice of its own salvation, *the ego balks*. Convincing itself that it's either become an illuminated adept and learned the awful truth about the reality of initiation, or that the reality of the path itself is in some way "evil," it recoils and wraps itself in a darker and deeper cloak of misfortune than ever before. Simply put, the individual comes face to face with their own truth, but they have not sufficiently destroyed their former ego-self, so they remain attached to it. They can now only see their true self as the enemy, and thereby evil. Crowley termed these individuals the Black Brothers, the counterpoint to the Great White Brotherhood of egoless adepts. The Black Brothers only see good and evil, and often little grey between, while those that successfully make the transition through the Abyss understand the subjectivity of good and evil—and that these ideas are in fact illusory.

All of this now allows us to understand the process of the Great Work as a whole.

The Great Work (Redux)

The great psychologist Carl Jung, in discussing alchemy, noted that its principal aim was "the ritual cohabitation of Sol and Luna." These luminaries represented in alchemical language the positive and negative, male and female. In psychological terms, they also represent the conscious and subconscious mind, an idea that brings us to the culmination of our discussion on the Great Work.

If we are in fact born as we were intended but are subsequently molded psychologically into someone that we are not, then what can be done to reverse that damage and rediscover ourselves? Stating this question a different way, if we are born such that our conscious and subconscious minds are in harmony, how do we restore our conscious mind to that same state of harmony? How do we bring about the "cohabitation of *sol* (conscious) and *luna* (subconscious)?"

If we look to the Abramelin Operation and its ultimate goal in the Knowledge and Conversation of the Holy Guardian Angel, this can be seen as fostering a personification of your "inner voice," which is itself allowing your subconscious mind a vehicle of expression. In short, you begin listening to the voice inside yourself that knows what is right for you and you alone, the voice that says who you truly are, absent of all external expectations—the one that has been there all along.

In this light, the HGA *is* your subconscious mind, and therefore the ultimate guide toward your *True Will*. What stands in the way of this full expression is the conscious mind, and in service to advancing that expression are the higher practices of raja yoga (among others) that seek to destroy the conscious mind. Once the conscious mind is destroyed, it can be reconstituted in the light of the subconscious, your *True Self*. This, then is the culmination of the Great Work, an individual who is uncompromisingly true to who they are and what they will to do in the world.

The Book of the Law

The book announces a New Law for mankind. It replaces the moral and religious sanctions of the past, which have everywhere broken down, by a principle valid for each man and woman in the world, and self-evidently indefeasible.

—*Magick*, Book 4, "The Summons"

Those who discuss the contents of this Book are to be shunned by all, as centres of pestilence.

—*The Book of the Law*, "The Comment"

No discussion of Thelema as either a spiritual philosophy or religious movement can be complete, or can truly even begin, without an understanding of the origins and canon—if one can call it such!—of *The Book of the Law*. There are several holy books in Thelema, originally released in three volumes, representing inspired works that define further the principles of the philosophy, but above them all stands *The Book of the Law*. It is the central text of Thelema and by its own instruction should be printed both in text and in facsimile—with holograph images of the manuscript included so that the style and placement of the letters as written might be consulted. "Change not as much as the style of a letter; for behold! thou, o prophet, shalt not behold all these mysteries herein."[85]

Each of *The Book of the Law*'s three chapters is related to a deity of the Egyptian pantheon: Nuit, Hadit, and Ra-Hoor-Khuit, respectively. "Why Egyptian?" one might ask, and rightly so. Well, Crowley's foundational symbol-set was in the traditions embraced by the Golden Dawn, which borrowed heavily from *en vogue* historical adaptations of Egyptology, the Egyptian *Book of the Dead*, and a general cultural fascination in the West. In more traditional associations, Nuit was the sky-goddess, and hence her elevation to all things celestial. To the ancients, the night "sky" in all its vastness was sufficient to denote that which was beyond the terrestrial. As we have evolved our understanding of the cosmos, we can now evolve our understanding of this deity as being the infinite universe. Hadit is less known and somewhat more difficult to define, but may be seen as a form of the solar deity. Ra-Hoor-Khuit is a form of Horus, who avenged the death of his father, Osiris, and is now the preeminent solar deity: hence *Ra*-Hoor, with the god Ra being the primary sun god.

The first chapter is given in the voice of the sky-goddess Nuit, the infinite universe, Great Mother, and embodiment of all potential experience. She is infinity as we most commonly think of it: vast and incomprehensible as the night sky. She declares that "Every man and every

---

85 Crowley, *The Book of the Law*, I:54.

woman is a star." Since Nuit is infinite, we can thus infer that every star is therefore the center of that infinite sphere. *Yes, you are actually the center of your own universe.* Crowley notes, "The old definition of God takes new meaning for us. Each one of us is the One God."[86] The Priestess in the Gnostic Mass echoes many of the words from this chapter, as a representation of the divine feminine.

The second chapter is dictated in the voice of Hadit, the Great Father and infinite contraction in reflection of Nuit's infinite expansion: he is the point within the infinite sphere. Confirming Nuit's assertion that she is the infinite circumference, he notes that, "In the sphere I am everywhere the center, as she, the circumference, is nowhere found."[87] He is the ultimate expression of selfhood in the midst of the infinitudes of possible experience. The open and loving phrases of the first chapter are now replaced with a significant trend toward realism: "I am Life, and the giver of Life, yet therefore is the knowledge of me the knowledge of death."[88] I would not go too far afield in suggesting that he represents the root of consciousness within the infinite scope of possible experience (Nuit): not the ego, which is a manifestation of that consciousness, but the actual psychological root that ultimately manifests the ego—Jung's concept of self. It is also in the second chapter that we get the Thelemic calendar of holy days, which will be treated more fully in the following section.

The third and final chapter is a fiery and emotional treatise in the voice of Ra-Hoor-Khuit, the same deity depicted in the Stele of Revealing, whose attitudes reflect in no uncertain terms the occasionally harsh realities and self-accountability of the Law of the Thelema. However, the understanding of these harsh realities is in service of the greater good of each and every star-consciousness. If Nuit represents the infinite scope of experience, or "universal consciousness," and Hadit represents the unique

---

86   Crowley, *The Commentaries of AL*, 4.

87   Crowley, *The Book of the Law*, II:3.

88   *Ibid.* II:6.

conscious (and unconscious) experience of the individual, then Ra-Hoor Khuit as the *magical child* of Nuit and Hadit represents the ego-experience of the individual—*that which goes*. "Nuit is your refuge as Hadit your light; and I am the strength, force, vigour, of your arms." [89] As a martial god, he speaks in terms of war and conflict, which is often difficult for readers to accept. Even Crowley had a great deal of difficulty accepting the final chapter of this work. It is doubtless challenging, but that should encourage you to seek what is beyond the words themselves. Few things worth finding are to be found at face value! Crowley notes that it took him five years to accept just the reasonably benign *first* chapter, never mind the last.

With such a brief synopsis of the work, you might think that I was trying to get away with avoiding any sort of commentary on *The Book of the Law*. You would be justified in thinking so, but it is actually well-meaning, because I do not want to craft your opinions of the work or the meaning of its content—at least not any more than I likely have already. One of the principal admonishments in "The Comment" at the end of *The Book of the Law*, of which it is part, though included much later, is that each and every person should endeavor to discover the meaning of *The Book of the Law* for themselves. One approach is to consider it an "open letter" to you personally. You may not understand all of it, and in fact may never, but over time you may come to understand something much greater: yourself.

Study it constantly.

FURTHER READING

The Book of the Law
The Holy Books of Thelema

---

89   Ibid., III:17.

The Aeon of Horus

One might think that Crowley would have siezed immediately upon such a powerful revelation as *The Book of the Law*, especially given the proofs demanded in the events leading up to it. However, this was not the case! He notes quite succinctly that, "Aiwass, in fact, was dictating to a hostile scribe." [90] It would be five years before he took up the manuscript again, discovering it in the attic of his Highland estate while searching for a pair of skis. Crowley's dedication to the establishment of the Aeon of Horus was about to begin in earnest—but what did that mean?

To answer that question, you must first understand the preceding aeons as Crowley understood them, which implies understanding the human conception of... well, conception! In fact, one must understand the ideas behind life and death as understood by the cultures in that time period, but the theory also hinges on the fact that over time the earth's regresses in its position relative to the signs of the Zodiac—one sign every two thousand years or so. Thus, each age represents and embodies nature of the sign in which it resides, giving it its character. [91]

The Aeon of Isis represents the time in human social development where life was seen to emerge solely from the mother, and it is thereby characterized by goddess and earth worship. Idealized, these communities would have been primarily engaged in deriving their subsistence from the earth as agrarian communities. The maternal had all the power to create, and from her all life was sustained. As far as they understood, the father had no part in the process of creation.

---

90   Crowley, *The Law is for All*, 13.

91   It is quite possible to assert that these concepts are extremely Eurocentric without fostering much of an argument, as the broad scope of cultures across the globe exist in varying states of social and economic development, but it was the Western context from which Crowley was approaching the idea. From that vantage, the idiosyncrasies of the explanation might be forgiven in pursuit of the understanding.

The Aeon of Osiris represents the paternal age of the last two thousand years, where it was the father that was seen to have and control the powers of procreation. It is also characterized by the masculine gods of death rather than the female goddesses of life, including the patriarchs of major religions such as Abraham, Mohammed, Jesus, and so on. It is also characterized by the idea of the slain and resurrected gods found in a number of cultures, such as Attis and Adonis, of which the Christian mythos is but one reflection. The mystery of life was now emboldened by the mystery of death, with the Egyptian conception of the sun's eternal rising and setting being the template long before the advent of this particular aeon. The father was now the supreme giver and taker of life, as can be seen in the attitudes prevailing before, and well into the transition period of, the Aeon of Horus.

The Aeon of Horus represents a balance between the maternal and paternal aspects, wherein both life and death are seen as natural complements. Consequently, both the masculine and feminine are seen as complements as well, neither being superior to the other. The nature of this aeon is that of both sexes combined, as is necessary in nature to create a new life (at least for us mammals).

If this seems a bit too far-fetched for you at a cosmic scale, that is entirely understandable, but consider that this same reflection can be made into the psyche of the individual as it emerges within the scope of a traditional family structure.[92] First, there is the mother as the sole sustaining force in the infant's life. Second, there is the paternal influence of provision outside of the mother, where the child now requires food from external sources traditionally gathered by the males of the "tribe." It is also the point at which the child recognizes his or her own mortality. Lastly, there is the emergence of the individual as a persona apart from either parent, the psychological severance from the parent in adulthood. The Aeon of Horus rejects such authoritarian dispensation from either

92   And admittedly, with traditional gender roles asserted as a generalization.

the maternal or paternal archetype: you are on your own now, free and independent.

The Beast and the Scarlet Woman

> Now ye shall know that the chosen priest & apostle of infinite space is the prince-priest the Beast; and in his woman called the Scarlet Woman is all power given. They shall gather my children into their fold: they shall bring the glory of the stars into the hearts of men.
>
> —*The Book of the Law*, I:15

Crowley famously quipped that his self-styled honorific of "The Beast" was a name his puritanical mother gave him—likely true! He delighted in his reputation for wickedness, but often with the *double entendre* that within that wickedness lay something much greater than mere degeneracy. In that seeming hedonism and whispers of "immoral" behavior lie the means to a real spiritual freedom in the hands of an accomplished adept. This was not always appreciated by his audiences, much less the yellow journalism of papers such as John Bull that would routinely spin up wild stories of "The Wickedest Man in the World."

But was he?

Crowley grew up in the repressive social climate of Victorian—and thereafter, Edwardian—England, an attitude exacerbated by his own family's adherence to the repressive religious strictures of the Plymouth Brethren. Even the briefest of introductions to his formative years shows a young man in the clutches of sadistic schoolmasters armed with the horrific might and malice of a self-righteous zealot acting with impunity. These conditions, always under the measure of religious propriety, nearly killed him—quite literally. Such a scenario certainly sets the scene for the Crowley we have come to know: a man who promulgated ideas of sexual freedom, mysticism, drug experimentation, and individual liberty in a rejection of contemporary social mores. That he would do so in such an outwardly scandalous fashion at times should equally come as no surprise.

The idea of "The Beast" is a reflection of the triumphant man that has overcome the petty morality of prevailing social attitudes in order to be true to himself. At the time, and even now, this was an overturning of the social order, especially when it came to sex. As a bisexual man in his time and age, to them, he *was* the Antichrist!

The idea of the Scarlet Woman, also taken of course from the biblical book of Revelation, is the feminine complement to the Beast. A title bestowed originally on his first wife, Rose, and later to some of his closest partners in the practice of sexual magick, it has the same connotations: a woman that has cast aside the social expectations of propriety with pride, joy, and—yes—lust!

Boleskine House

Boleskine is Crowley's former home and the direction toward which Thelemic rituals are performed unless otherwise specified. In this aspect, it serves as the "magical east" or a sort of "Thelemic Mecca" in establishing a current toward a particular location. Boleskine itself is an estate on the eastern shore of Loch Ness in Foyers, northern Scotland, approximately ten miles southwest of Inverness. Crowley originally purchased the estate during his time in the Golden Dawn as a suitably secluded location to perform the intense Abramelin work without interruption, but found that he equally enjoyed walking about the moors in all the trappings of a "Scottish laird." In all, he lived there nearly fifteen years, and he later designated the property to the Ordo Templi Orientis, the magical order he came to lead, including it in a small brochure with illustrative pictures as an enticement for prospective initiates.

Unfortunately, the house at Boleskine burned in December of 2015, and at the time of this writing there are no plans to restore it.

Qabalah

Given the importance of the foundations of Qabalah in Crowley's thought and writings, it is inescapable to discuss it in conjunction with him. It can well be said that Qabalah not only shaped his thought, but shaped *how* he thought. Thus, to understand Crowley, you must understand Qabalah, and not just a little. This is a daunting task, given the scope, complexity, and sublimity of the art.

Qabalah, also spelled Kabbalah or Cabala, originated as a method of Jewish mystical thought, which continues to be practiced in its traditional form even today. In the dawn of the European Renaissance, scholars took some of these ideas and incorporated them into the scope of Christian theology, both sanctioned and illicit, through work by early humanists such as Giovanni Pico della Mirandola and Johann Reuchlin. Pico's work attempted to resolve the philosophical basis of Qabalah, and subsequently Judaism, with that of Christianity, while Reuchlin had the slightly less ambitious goal of simply advocating for its merits. Naturally, neither was overly successful in the stern religious climate of a continent just then emerging from the Dark Ages.

Gematria

From a traditional Jewish standpoint, Qabalah is used to interpret religious texts, including what became known as part of the Old Testament in Christian theology—the Torah. Part of this practice included a method of analysis called *gematria.* The Hebrew letters being also numbers, you can sum the letters for a word or phrase to gain further insight, where words having a particular value are said to relate in some fashion. For instance, the Hebrew root for mother (AM) has a sum of 41 and father (AB) has a sum of 3. Combined, as in marriage, they would add to 44, which is the number of the Hebrew word for "blood," spelled with the Hebrew letters *DM*. Thus, one obtains an insight into family and the concept of generation by "blood relatives" through this analysis.

Similarly, one of the names of God used in the Torah is *Elohim*. In Hebrew letters, this word is spelled ALHIM, whose letters are numerically equivalent to 1, 30, 5, 10, and 40. If we look at the base numbers of 1, 3, 5, 1, and 4, then read backward starting at 3, we get 3.1415—an approximation of *pi*.[93] Of course, the connections that can be made are nearly infinite, but these examples begin to show the potency of these associations in building a set of interrelated symbols. Crowley also noted that *The Book of the Law* hid an expression of pi as well, to six digits.

Crowley was quite adept at gematria, and he elaborated on the process in *The Equinox, Vol. 1, No. 5*. He also consolidated much of the Qabalistic associations he learned from the Golden Dawn and elsewhere into his work *777*, which he describes as "a qabalistic dictionary of ceremonial magic, oriental mysticism, comparative religion and symbology."[94] In the eighth number of *The Equinox, Vol. 1*, he also included *Sepher Sephiroth*, a number dictionary of Qabalistically significant terms, originally compiled by his friend and mentor Allan Bennett. This includes the basic information on the alphanumeric associations of the Hebrew alphabet.

The Tree of Life

Perhaps most central to the Qabalah as it relates to the practice of ceremonial magick is a cosmological model known as the Tree of Life, which describes the creation and machinations of the universe in ten emanations known as *Sephiroth*, the singular of which is *Sephirah*. These are in fact also preceded by "negative veils of existence," called *Ain* (Nothingness), *Ain Soph* (Boundless Nothing), and *Ain Soph Aur* (Limitless Light). So, even before the universe came to be, there was a nothingness that filled all things and then became aware of itself—which then prompted the immediacy of existence: *cogito ergo sum*.

---

93   The method of numeric reduction here is known as the Qabalah of Nine Chambers, or AIQ BKR, where all numbers leading with the same digit are grouped and reduced to the root.

94   Crowley, *777 and Other Qabalistic Writings of Aleister Crowley*, vii.

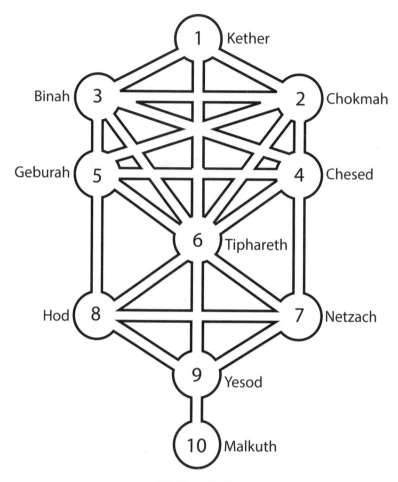

The Tree of Life

Emerging from the negative veils, the Tree of Life itself contains ten positive emanations, the Sephiroth.

No.	Sephirah	Meaning	Astronomy
1	Kether	Crown	First Swirlings
2	Chokmah	Wisdom	Zodiac
3	Binah	Understanding	Saturn

No.	Sephirah	Meaning	Astronomy
4	Chesed	Mercy	Jupiter
5	Geburah	Strength	Mars
6	Tiphareth	Beauty	Sun
7	Netzach	Victory	Venus
8	Hod	Splendor	Mercury
9	Yesod	Foundation	Moon
10	Malkuth	Kingdom	Earth (Elements)

These sephiroth define certain essential qualities as they descend from the highest and most abstract divine singularity in *Kether* to the base elemental sphere of *Malkuth*. These ten emanations are grouped into three triplicities, with the tenth and final sephirah representing the physical world being pendant to them. By the teachings of the Golden Dawn, the first three sephiroth are collectively known as the Supernal Triad, the next three the Ethical Triad, and the last three the Astral Triad.

The Four Worlds

Each of these triads, plus the final sephirah of Malkuth, also reflect a very important Qabalistic concept known as the Four Worlds. Similar to the manner in which the sephiroth themselves move from the highest divinity to the physical world, the concept of the Four Worlds divides the Tree of Life into four levels, or substrata, whereby the magnificence of the divine again manifests itself in the material world. The first of these "worlds," or phases of manifestation is the World of Archetypes, called *Atziluth*, represented by the Supernal Triad. The second is the World of Creation, called *Briah*, or *Beriah*, which brings the abstract concept from archetypal form into the stage of ideation. It is represented by the Ethical Triad. The third stage is the World of Formation, or *Yetzirah*, represented by the Astral Triad, which begins to shape the idea from Briah into specific form. Finally, the

fourth world, the World of Action, *Assiah*, represents the specific manifested instance of the form determined in Yetzirah.

Crowley considered the Qabalah a source of constant study and consistently recommended it to anyone wishing to study magick. Given the
intractable expanse of this sublime philosophical system, it is impossible to do it any reasonable justice within such a limited scope. In fact,
it would be difficult to do so within *any* limit of scope. It is a discipline
whose study is well rewarded, however. I can only offer the same suggestion, should you wish to come to terms with its view of the universe, and
ultimately your view of yourself within that universe.

FURTHER READING

The Mystical Qabalah (Dion Fortune)

The Chicken Qabalah (Lon Milo DuQuette)

777 and Other Qabalistic Writings of Aleister Crowley

Sepher Yetzirah

Sepher Ha-Bahir

The Zohar

Magical Formulæ of the New Aeon

For Crowley, magical formulæ were a means of expressing specific ideas in
a very concise form, and he would use many of them in ritual performances
to enhance or otherwise influence the understanding behind them. As
they will both lend an idea to the nature of Thelema and grant a better
understanding of the rituals presented hereafter, several of these formulæ
are described here. Some of the concepts are reasonably advanced, so do
not be troubled if you are unable to grasp them immediately!

The IAO Formula

Virgo, Isis, Mighty Mother. Scorpio, Apophis, Destroyer. Sol, Osiris, Slain and Risen. Isis. Apophis. Osiris. IAO!

—*The Golden Dawn,* Lesser Ritual of the Hexagram

IAO is actually an *old æon* formula: in fact, it is the principle formula of the Aeon of Osiris, the resurrected, phallic sun-god, into which category the major religions of the last few thousand years generally fall. These are the gods that—again, in a general sense—follow the Osirian myth of having sacrificed the phallus [95] either willingly, by accident, or by force. For instance, Osiris was killed and cut into pieces by his brother Set. His sister/wife Isis collected the pieces and restored him... except for the one piece that she couldn't find: his phallus. This solar deity thereafter became the lord of the underworld. We find equal stories of castration in the myth of Attis, the denial of the sexual function in Jesus, and many, many others. In fact, this latter concept of sex-denial has come to be associated with contemporary religious definitions of "moral behavior," so-called, which of course is at complete odds with natural behavior.

The three letters themselves, IAO, as defined by the adepts of Crowley's time, represent life, death, and resurrection—or the Egyptian gods Isis, Apophis, and Osiris. At its heart, the idea is that through a symbolic "death" via Apophis, we can emerge as something greater than we were previously—the *prima materia* represented in the natural state (Isis) is transmuted into the risen, supranatural Osiris. It is not a restoration of the former state, but a restoration to a *greater* state facilitated by this symbolic death or destruction.

---

95 Allegorically. Since the principal deities were male, this was the case. It should be understood as the sacrifice of the generative function, generally, whether male or female.

FIAOF

Crowley extended the IAO formula for the purposes of the Aeon of Horus, adding the Hebrew letter *vau* (*V*) equivalent to the Greek *stau* (*F*) to the beginning and end—bringing its numeration to 93 in alignment with the similar enumeration of *love* (Agape) and *will* (Thelema). He describes the nature of this new formula as follows:

- *F* (The Hierophant) is the manifested individual in its potency and possessed of creative force.
- *I* (The Hermit) is the *sperma* or root that is the unconscious Will.
- *A* (The Fool) is the blank slate, empty vessel, or host: the unmanifested child.
- *O* (The Devil) is the manifestation of the Will of *I* in the vessel of *O*, the enlightenment of the individual *F*.
- *F* (The Hierophant) having learned of his nature, if even a little.

If you are left wanting by Crowley's exposition above, you are not alone, so let us look at this idea a little more closely. Let's say you wish to create a sculpture from marble—no, not *wish*, you *will* to create a sculpture from marble. The possessor of the creative force (*F*) is you, and the Will (*I*) to create this sculpture has brought you to this large chunk of stone and the tools with which to work it (*A*). Working the stone, you finally create your masterpiece (*O*), and have likely learned more of your art through its practice, and more than a little about yourself (*F*). Thus, the entire process is one of self-illumination through experience.

There is a further and subtler secret in this formula in recognizing that the *I* and the *O* represent the male and female sexual organs, respectively, but it also speaks directly to the experience of initiation. We undergo an experience that changes us, in which case each experience is a "death" through which we emerge both the same and somewhat different than before, and hopefully somewhat the better. "Each such death is itself life, the means by which one realizes oneself in a series of episodes." [96] If one stops to consider the orgasm, or "little death," the formula's deeper meanings can be ascertained.

ABRAHADABRA

Abrahadabra; the reward of Ra-Hoor-Khuit.

—*The Book of the Law*, III:1

The formula expressed by the word *Abrahadabra* is fundamental in Thelema, so much so that it is considered the *Word of the Aeon*. It both begins and ends the third chapter of *The Book of the Law*, and is a variant on the older magical phrase *abracadabra*, which means "I create as I speak," symbolic of the Great Work, completed. So, what does *that* mean?

The phrase has a number of interesting numeric properties when studied in the light of gematria, a method of numerical analysis Crowley was keenly attuned to and on which he placed a great deal of importance. To start, *abrahadabra* has eleven letters, which brings us to the idea of five and six combined, the pentagram and the hexagram, man and god, thus the Great Work in that union. Reinforcing this idea, the letter *A* is represented five times, with six other diverse letters, where *A* is a representation of the pentagram, also called the *pentalpha—alpha* of course being the Greek letter *A*. So, again, we have the combination of the five and the six, once again inferring the Great Work.

The sum of its letters equals 418, which is also the value of the Hebrew letter *cheth* spelled in full, as "Ch I Th," *Cheth* (8), *Yod* (10), *Tau* (400). The letter is itself enumerated as 8, thus having implications to the initiatory current of the planet Mercury, which is traditionally associated to that number. Cheth is also the letter attributed to the Chariot card in the tarot, the bearer of the Holy Graal, which in turn is a reference to the idea of redemption: the bringing of a gross and impure thing to a higher state. The number 418 is also the enumeration of Ra-Hoor-Khuit. Such analysis could go on indefinitely.

---

96   Crowley, *Magick*, 167.

In *The Temple of Solomon the King*, Crowley's own account of his magical journey, he gives a detailed explanation of his own feelings regarding the manifold implications of this word, but leaves it at this: "... always the symbol will remain the Expression of the Goal and the Exposition of the Path." [97]

LASHTAL

Used within the ritual defined in *Liber V vel Reguli*, given hereafter, *Lashtal* embodies within itself the concept of "the all, the one, and the none."

LA is the Hebrew word for "nothing," or "naught," while the reverse of these letters, AL, is the name for God, all things, the omnipotent and eternal. Thus, the entire idea is book-ended by nothingness and every-thing-ness. Yet, as you may have guessed, there is more than this. If you consider a positive and negative, combined they make a neutral: a nothing, a naught. Thus, the concept of LA can also be seen as the union of Nuit and Hadit, Babalon and The Beast, conjoined—each lost in the other.

The combination of central letters *ShT* is pronounced *shet*, though not in the way you're likely laughing about presently—though the homophone is close enough! It is in fact another expression of the formula of the aeon, and representative of Ra-Hoor-Khuit himself. The letter *shin*, Sh, represents fire, and is associated with the Sun card in the tarot as well as having the literal meaning of "tooth," which is ultimately a weapon of destruction necessary to consume our food. [98] The letter *teth*, T, represents force, and is associated with the Strength card in the tarot, as well as implying a serpent by its shape. [99] ShT in combination, as force and fire, is then the dynamic expression of the all and the naught: it is action.

---

97   Crowley, *The Equinox*, I:V, 118.

98   Consider the use of the jawbone as a weapon in the hand of Samson.

99   Those familiar with Crowley's Thoth Tarot will object here, noting that he reverted Strength and Justice to their original positions by interposing them, then changing the name of the Justice card to Adjustment. However, Crowley notes in *Magick* specifically the image of the Strength card.

That's right—in the new aeon, life is ShT!

AUMGN

This word has been uttered by the **MASTER THERION** himself, as a means of declaring his own personal work as the Beast,
the *logos* of the Aeon.

—*Magick, Book 3*, Chapter VII

The word AUMGN was devised as an extension or improvement upon
AUM, also spelled OM, the Hindu mantra representing the full course
of breath and, ultimately, life. Crowley concluded that this was effectively an old aeon formula whose termination in the letter *M* implied
the attribution of the Hanged Man in the tarot, where "the formation
of the individual from the absolute is closed by his death." [100] Leverag-
ing the attributions of the major arcana of the tarot to improve upon
the idea, he included the letters *G*, the High Priestess, associated with
the flux of the moon, and *N*, Death, associated with ideas of regenera-
tion rather than the terminal *M* of the Hanged Man. This resulted in a
triune letter *MGN* that was affixed to the end of the word, as AUMGN,
"symbolizing thereby the subtle transformation of the apparent silence
and death which terminates the manifested life ... " [101] It is notable that
this compound letter MGN equates to 93, the same number as both *Agape*
(love) and *Thelema* (will).

In full, the word AUMGN equates to 100, which is a number of
perfection. It is also the enumeration of the Hebrew letter *qoph*, which
indicates the "back of the head" or subconscious. Its tarot card is Moon,
representing the manifested illusion through which we arrive at ... well,
existence! This new representation, pronounced no differently in practice given the "silent GN," now reflects the ebb and flow of manifestation rather than brute termination of life.

---

100 Crowley, *Magick*, 172.
101 Ibid., 153.

3

Practices and
Observations

As one might expect, the seemingly simple question of "What makes a Thelemite" can be difficult to answer, because the scope of beliefs and practices in Thelema are incredibly varied, based on the individual basis on which it rests. However, there are commonplace traditions and practices that originate with Crowley, which anyone interested in Thelema is likely to experiment with in exploring the scope of his work. Some are simple everyday observations, while others constitute a more elaborate basis of magical practice. How, when, where, and *if* you adopt any of these practices is of course up to you, but the following should give you a solid starting point to explore both the everyday observances and magical practices related to Thelema.

Each of these practices is presented in an increasing order of complexity, starting off with very simple everyday practices to integrate into your life as you see fit and to the degree that you feel comfortable. You do not have to start doing all of these practices at once, but I will suggest that you do them *exactly* as described herein, at least until you have a firm understanding of the principles. Otherwise you risk implicitly converting them into something more familiar to you and your current belief system. While it will feel more comfortable, it probably won't be Thelema: it will just be an expression of a different belief system adapted from Thelemic practice to conform to what you already believe, and that misses the point entirely.

If any of this feels uncomfortable at first—perhaps even frightening!—that is understandable. You are engaging in a new spiritual practice that likely challenges everything that you have ever known prior. To be a Thelemite you will need to challenge yourself to face these fears and these discomforts, rather than run from them as if they are "bad" or simply not for you. In a way, it is impossible for Thelema to not be for you, because Thelema is all about determining who you really are. However, if you decide after a while that you find other methods more appealing, I certainly can't argue with that. Just give each of these practices, each of which builds on the other, a fair chance first. I think you will find them beautiful, empowering, and helpful in the long run.

Thelemic Greetings

The phrases "Do what thou wilt shall be the whole of the Law," and "Love is the law, love under will," are the principal tenets of Thelemic philosophy and culture. Both of these phrases appear in *The Book of the Law*, and as a means of keeping them constantly in mind, Crowley urged their use in everyday communications. Even in the last of his days, he would greet people with an enthusiastic "Do what thou wilt shall be the whole of the Law!"

Today, Thelemites commonly use a shortened version of this greeting as "93," referring to the equivalent enumeration of the Greek words for *love* (Agape) and *Will* (thelema). Thus, in meeting, it is common to say "93" instead of "hello" or "goodbye" rather than the more cumbersome exchange of the full phrase "Do what thou wilt shall be the whole of the Law," and so on. This was also something Crowley would do, especially in correspondence.

In formal written communications, however, it is customary to begin the correspondence with the full "Do what thou wilt shall be the whole of the Law," and complete the correspondence with, "Love is the law, love under will."

Thus, a formal letter might look like the following:

Mr. Neuberg,

Do what thou wilt shall be the whole of the Law. I would like to thank you for your kind hospitality last Saturday. It was a very enjoyable time, and I hope to meet with you again soon.

Love is the law, love under will.

Aleister

However, for informal correspondence, it is more common to use "93" as well, but in a slightly different form:

Vic,

93
Thanks for having me over the other night. Let's do it again!

93 93/93
Aleister

The expression of "93 93/93" in closing refers to the same line as before, "Love is the law, love under will." The division of 93/93 is a clever device for expressing love (Agape) "under" will (Thelema).

So, do you just start yelling "93" at everyone you meet? That much is up to you, but generally speaking, the use of greetings is exchanged between people who know each other to be Thelemites, and not in everyday exchanges like at the workplace, etc. In *Magick Without Tears*, Crowley notes, "I don't think it good manners to force my idiosyncrasies down people's throats, and I don't want to appear more eccentric than I need.

silence

It might detract from my personal influence, and so actually harm the Work that I am trying to perform."[102]

Sage advice, indeed.

Saying Will

Similar to the custom of saying "93" in greeting or departing, saying "Will" before eating and drinking is also a custom observed by Thelemites when dining together. It consists of a call-and-response, where one person leads the call, and the others reply in the following manner:

blessing of the food

Leader: [knocks] Do what thou wilt shall be the whole of the Law!

Other(s): What is thy will?

Leader: It is my will to eat and drink!

Other(s): To what end?

Leader: That I may fortify my body thereby!

Other(s): To what end?

Leader: That I may accomplish the Great Work!

Other(s): Love is the law, love under will!

Leader: [knocks] Fall to!

This simple exchange is similar to saying "grace" before meals as observed in many religious traditions. Similar to the use of "93" in greeting, it serves to reinforce the dedication of the participants to the accomplishment of the Great Work and establishment of Thelema within the course of their own lives. When dining alone, you can also perform the entire exchange by yourself, answering your own questions as a reminder of your personal dedication toward that end. It also serves to make the

---

102   Crowley, *Magick Without Tears*, 151.

meal a Eucharistic rite, in that the consumption of food is aimed toward the greater purpose of fulfilling the ultimate will of each participant.

The Magical Diary

We know quite a bit about Crowley's life not only because of his own auto-hagiography, but also because of his exceptional habit of keeping a daily diary. Yes, there are spots where he was less diligent than others, much as anyone might find about keeping a daily diary, but he was quite fastidious as a rule. So great was his belief in keeping a diary that he made it a requirement for even the *probationers* of his magical order, the A∴A∴. Not only was it a good practice, he considered it fundamental to the progress of the initiate.

Aside from keeping a daily record of your life, Crowley notes that you should give an account of your life to date. Where were you born? Under what circumstances, and to whom? What was your childhood like, and so on into adulthood. Once this is in place, *then* you are ready to begin your daily work. It need not be exhaustive, but it should be accurate, and leave out no details that come to your mind. Crowley even notes that you should detail anything you recall *before* your birth! That would include images or memories from past lives, whether or not you believe in such a thing.

Crowley states several items that may be included in the diary in a prefix to *Liber E*, a work on the development of clairvoyant abilities, the practice of yoga, and the recording of such experiments. [103] As a suitable example, he cites his own exhaustive diary in "John St. John," originally published as a special supplement to *The Equinox, Vol. 1, No. 1*. [104] We can thus use a few lines to instruct us in the proper form, though it is clear in this case that a surplus of time was at his disposal, set aside for the purpose of these operations. To wit, he had set himself on a study of the

---

103   Crowley, *Magick*, "Liber E vel Exercitorium sub figura IX," 593.

104   Crowley, *The Equinox, Vol. 1, No. 1*, Special Supplement, 1–139.

practices of controlling the mind—rather, *thought*—and sought to do so under the same conditions that someone of ordinary means might do. There were no trips to mountaintops or exotic locations. No, it was Paris in which he found himself, which is exotic enough for some...

Oct 1. The First Day

At Eight o'clock I rose from sleep and putting on my Robe, began a little to meditate. For several reasons—the journey and business of the day before, etc. etc., I did not feel fresh. But forcing myself a little I rose and went out to the Café du Dôme [105] where I took coffee and a brioche, after buying an exercise book in which to write this record.

This was about *8.45*; and now (*10.10*) I have written thus far.

10.45 I have driven over to the Hammam [106] through the beautiful sunshine, meditating on the discipline of the Operation.

It seems only necessary to cut off definitely dispersive things, aimless chatter and such; for the Operation itself will guide one, leading to disgust for too much food and so on. If there be upon my limbs any chain that requires a definite effort to break it, perhaps sleep is that chain. But we shall see—*solvitur ambulando*. [107] If any asceticism be desirable later on, true wariness will soon detect any danger, and devise a means to meet it and overcome it.

12.0 Have finished bath and massage, during which I continued steadily but quite gently, "not by a strain laborious and hurtful

---

105   Crowley was in Paris at the time, and this café was a popular gathering place for expatriates in the Montparnasse area.

106   A "hammam" is a Turkish bath.

107   A Latin phrase meaning, "It is solved by walking."

but with stability void of movement," [108] willing the Presence of Adonai.

12.5 I ordered a dozen oysters and a beefsteak, and now (12.10) find myself wishing for an apple swallowed and chewed by deglutition, [109] as the Hatha Yogis do. The distaste for food has already begun.

12.12 Impressions already *failing to connect.*

I was getting into Asana [110] and thinking, "I will record this fact," when I saw a jockey being weighed. I thought of recording *my own* weight which I had not taken.

Good!

12.13 Pranayama [10 seconds to breathe in, 20 seconds to breathe out, 30 seconds to hold the breath.] Fairly good; made me sweat again thoroughly. Stopped not from fatigue but from lunch.

[Odd memoranda during lunch. Insist on pupils writing down their whole day; the play as well as the work. "By this means they will become ashamed, and prate no longer of 'beasts.'"]

I am now well away on the ascetic current, devising all sorts of privations and thoroughly enjoying the idea.

12.55 Having finished a most enjoyable lunch, will drink coffee and smoke, and try to get a little sleep. Thus to break sleep up into two shifts.

2.18 A nice sleep. Woke refreshed.

---

108   A quote not from any yogic text, but from *The Chaldean Oracles of Zoroaster.*

109   "Swallowing."

110   A posture used in the practice of yoga.

3.15 Am arrived home, having performed a little business and driven back.

Will sit down to do Asana, etc.

3.20 Have started.

3.28 7 Pranayama[III] cycles enough. Doubtless big lunch is a nuisance.

I continue meditating simply.

3.36 Asana hurts badly, and I can no longer concentrate at all. Must take 5 minutes' rest and then persevere.

Of course, the diary goes on, but you can glimpse even from this the exhaustiveness of a true "magical diary" in practice. Crowley shows an inclusion not only of the spiritual pursuits that he was undertaking, but also the minor details of daily life—you never know when one might connect to the other!

In personal practice, the contents of the diary, aside from your general activities, should include the date and time, astrological conditions (if relevant), weather, mood, ideas you may be considering, and especially the results of any magical practices you have engaged in. It is especially important to note the outcome of your magical work *immediately after completing it* to ensure as true an account as possible. The memory is quite skilled in adapting the recollection of events, subtly and not-so-subtly re-storying the entire affair. The closer to the event, as well as pen and paper, the more accurate your record will be.

The Thelemic Calendar

The vernal equinox on March 20th is the start of the new year in Thelema, aligning the year with the course of the zodiac that begins anew in

---

III   Yogic breathing exercises, as described in the earlier passage at 12.13.

Aries and the emergence of spring in the Northern Hemisphere. Each year is "counted" based on the major arcana of the tarot in major cycles of twenty-two years, with a "zero" date of the Equinox of the Gods, March 20, 1904, the transition from the Aeon of Osiris to the Aeon of Horus. This is much like the Gregorian calendar, which has an inception date of the (alleged) birth of Christ for its basis.

Each year's designation is based on a card in the major arcana of the tarot, indicated by the Roman numeral of that card. Thus, every year the "minor" counter advances by one, but every twenty-two years, the "major" counter increases by one and the minor counter becomes zero again—just like the single digits place becomes zero when you reach ten. As an example, on March 20, 2015 (of the Common Era), the Thelemic year transitioned from V.i to V.ii—representing the Hierophant with the Roman numeral five (major) and sequentially the Magus and the High Priestess with the Roman numerals one and two (minor).

Since the basis of the year is astrological, it is also common to note the date and time using the astrological positions of the sun and the moon. For example, the date and time of an event—even so simple as the time of writing of a letter—might be represented as ☉ 12° ♈ and ☽ 23° ♌, the sun in twelve degrees Aries and the moon in twenty-three degrees Leo, which gives the astrological conditions under which the event occurred. It is important to note that this scheme is not used in everyday life to "tell time." It would be not only cumbersome—"Can you come over at Q 12° A, R 23° E?"—but lacks the sense of precision required to reasonably schedule anything!

Holy Days

Are there Thelemic holidays? In fact, yes—a number of them. Many of these derive from *The Book of the Law* and the circumstances surrounding its reception, but also in denoting the major events in the life of a Thelemite: birth, puberty, death, and so on. Other holidays have been included over the years as unofficial observances, but commonly celebrated nonetheless—such as Crowley's own birth and death.

The *Book of the Law* defines the canon of the religious calendar of Thelema in the second chapter, verses 36–43:

> *There are rituals of the elements and feasts of the times.*
> *A feast for the first night of the Prophet and his Bride!*
> *A feast for the three days of the writing of the Book of the Law.*
> *A feast for Tahuti and the child of the Prophet—secret, O Prophet!*
> *A feast for the Supreme Ritual, and a feast for the Equinox of the Gods.*
> *A feast for fire and a feast for water; a feast for life and a greater feast for death!*
> *A feast every day in your hearts in the joy of my rapture!*
> *A feast every night unto Nu, and the pleasure of uttermost delight!*

Feasts of the Times

As a natural and recurring observation of the sun's course throughout
the year, it is quite common for Thelemites to celebrate the solstices
and equinoxes as "feasts of the times." Crowley notes that "... the entry
of the Sun into the cardinal signs of the elements at the Equinoxes and
Solstices are suitable for festivals." [112]

The Prophet and His Bride

A "feast for the first night of the Prophet and his Bride" refers to the wedding date of Aleister Crowley and Rose Kelly on August 12. Rose was of
course the Scarlet Woman through whom Crowley was led to the revelation
of *The Book of the Law*, and this date is meant to commemorate that union.

The Three Days

A "feast for the three days of the writing of the Book of the Law" is self-
explanatory and typically celebrated over the course of the three days of
its reception on April 8, 9, and 10. A common custom is to read each
chapter on the day it was received, with a celebration at noon.

---

112   Crowley, *The Commentaries of AL*, 131.

A Feast for Tahuti

"A feast for Tahuti and the child of the Prophet—secret, O Prophet" is ... well, secret! There is no associated date with its celebration, and Crowley notes, "This particular feast is of a character suited only to initiates." [113] As is often the case with Crowley's comments to this effect, it is an allusion to the practice of sex magick.

The Supreme Ritual

A "feast for the Supreme Ritual" is celebrated on March 20 in commemoration of Crowley's invocation of Horus that led to his reception of *The Book of the Law*.

The Equinox of the Gods

The "feast for the Equinox of the Gods" is celebrated on the vernal equinox in commemoration of the announcement, by way of the Supreme Ritual, that Horus had taken the place of Osiris and that a New Aeon had been set in motion. It also occurs on March 20, and is generally celebrated in concert with the Supreme Ritual.

Fire and Water

The "feast for fire" and "feast for water" are celebrations of the coming-of-age for boys and girls, respectively—when they reach puberty. It thus represents a similar observation to the Jewish bar or bat mitzvah.

Life

A "feast for life" is for the birth (and birthday) of a Thelemite. It also has given rise to one of two more commonly celebrated noncanonical holidays, the birth date of Aleister Crowley on October 12, on which his Lesser Feast is celebrated—as opposed to the Greater Feast for death. Thelemites also

---

113   Crowley, *The Commentaries of AL*, 131. (Commentaries of this kind generally imply that the practice is related to sex magick.)

speak of one's "solar return" when referring to a birthday, since the Earth has circled the sun one more time since they were born.

Death

A "feast for death" is of course the celebration of death. It has given rise to the second noncanonical holiday, the date of Crowley's death, December 1, on which his Greater Feast is celebrated. It is important to note that death is celebrated in Thelema as a natural course and result of having lived in the first place. Gone are the days of fear and distress at the approach of the inevitable. "It is of the utmost importance to make funerals merry, so as to train people to take the proper view of death." [114]

Calendar

Allowing for celebrations of singular life-events, the full scope of the annual calendar (to which your own birthday may be added!) is thus:

Holiday	Date
Spring Equinox	March 20
Supreme Ritual	March 20
Equinox of the Gods	March 20
Three Days	April 8, 9 & 10
Summer Solstice	June 20
First Night	August 12
Fall Equinox	September 21
Crowley's Lesser Feast (Birth)	October 12
Crowley's Greater Feast (Death)	December 1
Winter Solstice	December 21

---

114   Crowley, *The Commentaries of AL.* Ed. by Marcelo Ramos Motta 132.

Yoga

"…if a chance thought can produce much effect, what cannot fixed thought do?"

—*Liber Libræ* vel XXX

Aided by the influence of his early friend and mentor in magick Allan Bennett, as well as his friend and mentor in mountaineering, Oscar Eckenstein, Crowley became an ardent proponent of yoga, and specifically a branch known as raja yoga. Unlike much of the modern practice of yoga, which focuses on a series of postures designed to promote greater health and well-being, raja yoga is focused on *mental* discipline and the resultant spiritual attainment. However, in order to begin that mental work, we first need to conquer the distractions of the physical body. Only then can we begin turning inward to our thoughts and emotions to begin the long process of introspection that leads us to further and greater attainments.

Yama & Niyama

These two pillars of yoga are purely ethical, being the exercise of right thought and right action in things that should be avoided (yama) and things that should be engaged in (niyama).

In traditional practice, yama consists of the following injunctions: not killing, not stealing, not receiving gifts, not being dishonest, and avoidance of excess. The intent of their observation is simple: to ensure that the mind is not disturbed, especially by thoughts of negativity, anxiety, and so forth. Crowley notes particularly that common sense should be the guide throughout their observance, and that each person should endeavor to define their own code *and stick to it*.

Niyama is less adequately defined, and different texts define them differently in type and number. The sage Patanjali, as close as we might hope to find in a master of the practice, notes them as purity, contentment, discipline, introspection, and contemplation. These all seem fairly reasonable aspirations, but they are based on a cultural context that may not be suited to the individual temperament. As in *yama*, the idea is to start here and work out what least disturbs the mind—developing a truly "clear conscience," as it were.

In short, if both yama and niyama are to serve in quieting the mind, then their practice must be steered toward a course that does not cause a "troubled" mind, each principle in service to the character of the individual. There is thus no set of discrete principles that can be applied as definitive, and so it is left to each individual to determine through experience which things upset their psyche, at which point those things should be avoided. This introspective practice alone is of no small value to the practitioner, as it begins to point the individual toward his or her true sense of self through acknowledgment of what things cause them distress (or excitement) and what things do not.

Asana

"The first difficulty arises from the body, which keeps on asserting its presence by causing its victim to itch, scratch, and other ways to be distracted." [115]

The very first practice in yoga is that of posture, or *asana*, for which Crowley quotes the yogi Patanjali in stating, "... asana is that which is firm and pleasant." We are thus able to grasp the idea immediately: any steady posture that does not cause significant strain. Its goal is to allow the mind to be free of the myriad distractions that the body produces, be they a simple itch, the twitch of a muscle, and so on. This is unfortunately more easily said than done.

While modern yoga for exercise has a number of asanas that one transitions through in the course of a session, raja yoga is different: you pick one position and you stay in it. Thus, an asana for our purposes may be as simple as sitting upright in a chair, or cross-legged, or kneeling, or in some other "firm" position that allows the weight of the body to be supported without significant muscle strain ... at least at first. While

---

115 Crowley, *Magick*, 15.

starting out, the practitioner may question why everyone makes such a fuss over sitting still, but one finds quite quickly that the simple act of stillness can be quite difficult! Even the slightest of tensions becomes unbearable after a relatively short time, never mind the occasional itch that *just won't seem to go away*. Crowley notes, correctly, that one should not be surprised early on to find that quitting the posture may equally produce several minutes of the most acute agony, as well.

Despite these difficulties, he also notes that under no circumstance should you try another posture once you've begun this practice. You may choose to try several postures in the beginning, but once you select the asana that works for you, stick to it! No progress will be gained by changing to a "better" asana just when things start to get difficult. Eventually, you will find that the posture becomes quite simple again, and your asana allows you to master the nagging impulses of your body as you begin your meditations.

Pranayama

Prana is the term for the life force, and is connected with the breath; pranayama therefore is the control of the breath. It should be practiced in conjunction with asana, as each greatly supports the practice of the other. There are a myriad number of specialized practices that include the blocking of one nostril or another in this control of the breath, the scope of which is too broad to enter into here. At a basic level, inhaling for four "counts," exhaling for an equal measure, and then holding the breath for twice that (eight counts), is sufficient. Each count must be equal, as there is a definite tendency to accelerate the counts as one runs out of breath! It is also vitally important to ensure you do not strain your lungs in this practice. Do not breathe in or out too much; at the completion of the exhalation, the body should be relaxed and supported by the weight of your asana.

Crowley also connects this practice with *mantrayoga*, the constant repetition of phrases that help prevent the mind from wandering. The most famous of these is the simple "aum," but more complicated phrases may be used should you find that the repetition of "aum" allows your mind to wander down other paths. Even counting, as noted above in measuring the course of the breath, may be a sufficient mantra. "Aum mani padme hum" is another classic mantra, but it can literally be any phrase that you can repeat such that it sticks in the mind: "Do what thou wilt shall be the whole of the Law," "Love is the law, love under will," "Abrahadabra," and so on.

You may find over time that the phrase you select will "speed up" or begin to repeat at a faster and faster pace in your mind, taking on a life of its own. You may even find yourself well off on another complex train of thought entirely without even noticing it, yet your mantra has remained unbroken! This is a good indicator, but further work will need to be done to retain the focus solely on the mantra itself.

Pratyahara

Now that the posture and breath are taken care of, we can turn our attention inward in the first purely mental practice of the art: *pratyahara*. This practice begins the observation of thoughts as they arise in the mind, many of which go unnoticed because they are so fleeting. Crowley notes that just as the body was found to be endlessly restless once observed, so the mind shall prove to be—and yet more so.

The idea behind pratyahara is thus to control the thoughts. As one begins, a great number of thoughts whirl by, but the aim at first is simply to observe them without (emotional) reaction. A thought passes, and it is gone; then another, and another. As each thought passes the chaotic swirl of thought-stuff that was your mind begins to unwind, and you begin to find fewer and fewer thoughts to deal with. You begin to feel, perhaps finally, at peace. This is when you may begin the next practice: *dharana*.

Dharana

When most people think of meditation, they are actually inferring contemplation. Here, we imply *concentration*, which is a very different animal indeed. Dharana is the focusing of the mind on one thought, and one thought only, without diversion. We do this with relative frequency when we get "wrapped up" in something that demands our intellectual attention at its fullest, but it is decidedly less easy when the subject of our attention becomes less complex. You may find it quite easy to become involved in a difficult math equation for several minutes, thinking of nothing else—but what happens when you try to imagine a small white circle? It steadies for a moment, then varies in size, elongates, wobbles, changes color, flips about, and any number of other gymnastics seemingly impossible to its geometry!

One should begin this practice already seated and established in a sound asana. Crowley adds a pencil, note paper, and stopwatch nearby such that you may mark the number of "breaks" that occur when attempting to think only upon that simple object. (The white circle was merely an example. It can be anything.) Ten minutes should be sufficient to start, marking each time the mind strays from its object. In many cases, you may find yourself several minutes down a secondary train of thought without even realizing it. The aim is to increase concentration, with fewer and fewer marks as one progresses.

Dhyana

"The most important factor in dhyana is ... the annihilation of the Ego." [116]

We now reach the state of yoga that is less a practice than a result, but whose achievement stems from a consistent practice in dharana. Ultimately, the focus of the mind upon the object is such that one no longer distinguishes the between two. If this sounds a bit mystical, you're right! Even Crowley struggled to come to terms in describing the experience of *dhyana*: "It is indescribable even by the masters of language; and it is

---

116 Crowley, *Magick,* 32.

therefore not surprising that semi-educated stutterers wallow in oceans of gush." [117] I shall nonetheless try my best!

If we consider dharana as the unbroken focus upon the object in question, where we have trained the mind to bear an unwavering connection to its observation, then dhyana is when we've managed to do this so expertly that we forget *ourselves*. The subjective experience of the object—that is, your perception of the object as something separate from yourself—falls away in a thunderous silence. On first experience, it comes as such a great shock that you will likely fall out of your trance immediately! However, practice and experience will once again allow you to prolong *this* state as well, much as you did in the mental concentration of dharana.

Samadhi

Dharana is the holding of the mind to some particular object. An unbroken flow of knowledge about that object is dhyana. When that (i.e. dhyana) gives up all forms and reveals only the meaning, it is Samadhi.

—Swami Vivekananda [118]

Samadhi is considered to be the pinnacle of achievement in raja yoga. It is in a sense an extension and continuation of the attainment found in dhyana, but yet more than that—and if so much rubbish has been written about dhyana, I hardly stand a chance to describe the "ultimate union of all things," the existent and the nonexistent all at once!

Crowley notes that in dhyana even the concepts one is focused on in achieving this state have a form and idea behind them. Samadhi destroys these boundaries just as dhyana destroyed the difference between subject (the observer) and object (the observed). "Not only are all forms and ideas destroyed, but also those conceptions which are implicit in our

---

117   Crowley, *Magick*, 31.

118   Vivekananda, *Raja-Yoga*, 183.

ideas of those ideas." [119] Crowley makes the analogy of a candle in a darkened room, whose light is made irrelevant by the opening of the shutters and its "annihilation" by the overwhelming rays of the sun. This, perhaps, is then the idea of samadhi: the union of the One as indistinguishable from the All.

FURTHER READING
Magick (Part One: Mysticism)

Raja-Yoga by Vivekananda

The Shiva Samhita

The Hatha Yoga Pradipika

The Basics of Thelemic Ritual

Many of the basics of magical ritual in general can be found in Crowley's *Liber O vel Manus et Saggitae sub figura VI*. (I know: it's a long and eccentric title.) It is essentially a primer for magical practice gleaned from his time in the Golden Dawn, including pentagram rituals, hexagram rituals, the assumption of god forms, and a wealth of advice for the aspiring student. In order to have a firm understanding of the ritual practices of Thelema, we will tackle each of these in turn.

Pentagrams

Perhaps nothing is more closely associated with magick in modern practice than the image of the pentagram, the five-pointed star. From Greek magic and sacred geometry to its use in medieval magical ritual and its modern-day association with both Wicca and Satanism, the pentagram has an equal place of prominence in Thelema. For Crowley, the pentagram represented the *microcosm*, or individual. Drawing on its associations with spirit as the fifth element binding together the four traditional elements

---

119 Crowley, *Magick*, 41.

of earth, air, fire, and water, it can also be understood as a symbol of any (and every) man or woman.

Modern magical practice associates the pentagram with the elements starting with spirit at the uppermost point. The upper right point is associated with water, the lower right with fire, the lower left with earth, and the upper left with air. Using this arrangement, you can *invoke* (increase or draw toward) or *banish* (decrease or push away) the energies of a particular element, which means to either increase or decrease their influence or potential within the scope of a ritual. As an example, the Lesser Banishing Ritual of the Pentagram, perhaps the best known and most used ritual originating from the Golden Dawn, uses the banishing pentagrams for the element of earth to clear away any mundane or otherwise unwanted energies.

The elemental pentagram

In fact, much of what we have come to understand as a "traditional" arrangement of the pentagrams with respect to invoking and banishing comes from the work of the Golden Dawn, who included this information in their teachings. In their system, they devised four invoking and four banishing pentagrams, each determined by where the person started drawing the figure and in what direction. For example, starting at the uppermost point and beginning the figure by tracing the line down and to the left, moving in a counterclockwise direction, you are drawing the invoking pentagram of the element of earth. The banishing pentagram begins on the opposite end of that same line, beginning at the lower left point and moving clockwise toward the uppermost point. They also included four different pentagrams for spirit: an active and passive invoking and an active and passive banishing to correlate to the active (fire, air) and passive (earth, water) elements, respectively. [120]

Among many, many other ritual practices, pentagrams are used in the Star Ruby, itself based on the Lesser Banishing Ritual of the Pentagram, and in *Liber V vel Reguli*, both of which are detailed hereafter.

Hexagrams

The Red Triangle is the descending tongue of grace; the Blue Triangle is the ascending tongue of prayer.

—The Book of Lies, Chapter 69

We often see hexagrams in the context of Jewish mysticism and religious practice, typically in the form of two interlocking triangles familiarized as the Star of David. It is also well entrenched in the Western magical tradition. As a compliment to the five-sided star that indicates the microcosm, the six-sided star represents the *macrocosm*, or god.

While the points of the pentagram are elemental, the points of the hexagram are related to the seven planets known by the ancients: Saturn, Jupiter, Mars, the Sun, Venus, Mercury, and the Moon. The uppermost point is related to Saturn, then Jupiter on the upper right, Mars on the upper left, Venus on the lower right, Mercury on the lower left, and finally the Moon on the lowermost point.

---

120 Regardie, *The Golden Dawn*, 280–284. (The author does not necessarily assert his agreement with this system of drawing the pentagrams, but presents it for context.)

You'll notice that I left out one "planet"—the Sun! It is placed in the center of the hexagram.

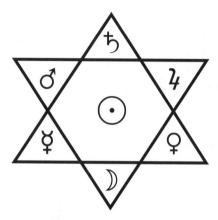

The planetary hexagram

Crowley is famous for his use of the _unicursal hexagram,_ meaning a hexagram drawn using only one line—with a "line" being defined as a figure drawn without lifting the pen from the paper—rather than the two lines used in traditional pentagrams, each forming a separate triangle. This is accomplished as shown in the following figure:

The unicursal hexagram

This figure is often depicted with a flower having five petals in the very center where its inner arms intersect, representing the microcosm, (man) within the surrounding hexagram of the macrocosm (god). In this form, it is representative of the Great Work complete—the union of god and man.

God Forms and Signs

Within the rituals of Thelema, as in many rituals from modern ceremonial magick, the assumption of so-called "god forms" is intended to attune the practitioner to the postures, energies, and attitudes of that deity within a ritual setting. In so doing, they provide a powerful complement to standard ritual practice, which not only enhances the nature of ritual but can also be an effective practice in their own right. The following god forms or signs are used in a number of rituals that will be discussed herein, so we gather them here for reference.

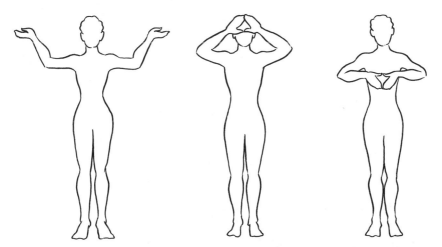

The elemental signs (from left to right): air, fire, water

SHU (AIR)

Named after the Egyptian sky-goddess who holds up the heavens, this posture is given by standing perfectly erect, holding the arms above the head, and with bent elbows turning the hands inward and facing up as if to support the sky. The feet are held together.

THOUM-AESH-NEITH (FIRE)

With the feet together, flatten the hands against the forehead and place them together such that only the tips of the index fingers and tips of the thumbs touch, making a triangle pointing upward in the empty space between them, the palms facing outward.

AURAMOTH (WATER)

This is the same posture as the previous, Thoum-aesh-neith, but with the palms inward and the hands forming a triangle at the level of the solar plexus. Again, the feet are together.

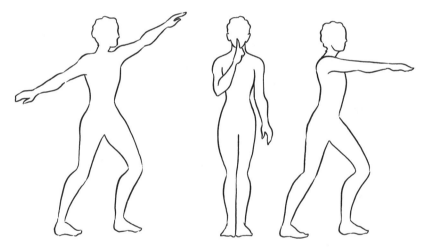

The elemental signs continued (from left to right): earth, silence, enterer

SET (EARTH)

The sign of Set is given by advancing the right foot and raising the straightened right arm so that the hand, palm down, is above the shoulder, the left arm straightened and angled behind the body at about the same angle.

Harpocrates (Silence)

This sign, representing Hoor-paar-Kraat, also known as Harpocrates or Horus the infant, is given by standing straight, feet together, and placing the extended forefinger of the right hand (the other fingers closed) against the lower lip, as if to say, "Quiet!" The left hand remains at your side.

Horus (The Enterer)

The Sign of the Enterer is given by thrusting the open hands outward at the level of the eyes while simultaneously stepping forward with the left foot. It is the active and projective form of Horus, as opposed to the passive or withdrawn form observed in the Sign of Silence.

The Signs of L.V.X.

The signs of L.V.X., pronounced *looks* and meaning "light" in Latin, are a series of signs usually given in conjunction with one another. They consist of signs related to the Egyptian gods Isis, Typhon, and Osiris, and follow the passion play of Osiris in Egyptian mythology through life, death, and rebirth. Sound familiar? This is another expression of the IAO formula!

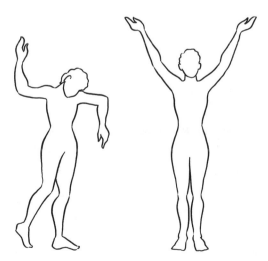

The signs of L.V.X. (from left to right): Isis Mourning (L), Apophis (V)

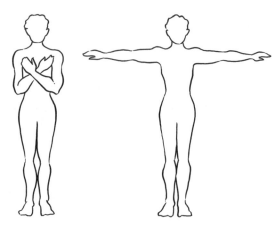

The signs of L.V.X. continued (from left to right): Osiris Risen (X), Osiris Slain

THE SIGN OF ISIS MOURNING

This sign represents the *L* of L.V.X. and is therefore the first in succession. It is also known as the swastika, which of course long predates its now nefarious connections in the West. It represents the swirling forces of creation with which Isis can be identified. Standing upright, turn the body sideways such that the left leg is straight (bearing weight) and the right is behind and bent at an angle such that only the toes are touching the floor. Both arms are held out in line with the shoulders, the right arm bent upward at the elbow at ninety degrees, the left arm bent downward at the elbow ninety degrees. The head is bowed.

THE SIGN OF APOPHIS

Related to the great and terrible serpentine Nile-god, this is a destructive energy and related to the *V* of L.V.X. Standing upright and with the feet together, raise both arms above your head at forty-five degree angles, respectively, holding them in the shape of a *V*. It is also referred to as the Sign of Typhon, who is a monstrous Greek deity, and each represents a principal challenger or enemy of the primary god (Ra, Zeus, etc.).

THE SIGN OF OSIRIS RISEN

Completing the cycle, the third sign represents the risen/resurrected Osiris, representing the *X* of L.V.X. It is given by standing upright and crossing the arms, right over left, the hands held flat against the shoulders or upper body.

THE SIGN OF OSIRIS SLAIN

A fourth and final sign, not related to one of the letters, is that of the slain Osiris. Standing upright, the arms are held out horizontally in line with the shoulders as if to make a cross. The feet are together.

THE SIGNS OF N.O.X.

N.O.X., pronounced *knocks* and meaning "night" in Latin, stands for the "Night of Pan," the point at which the ego-self is destroyed. This idea is elaborated in verse form in one of the Holy Books, *Liber VII*, and briefly in chapter 1 of *The Book of Lies*. In full, their sequence suggests the conception and birth of a child.

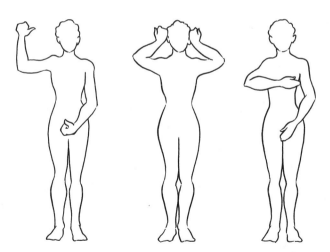

The signs of N.O.X. (from left to right): Puer, Vir, Puella

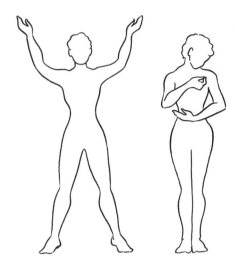

The signs of N.O.X. continued (from left to right): Mulier, Mater Triumphans

PUER (BOY)

The first sign is *Puer*, which is a young boy. The right hand, thumb extended, is raised such that the shoulder and elbow are both at ninety-degree angles. The left hand, thumb also extended, is placed at the genitals to represent the phallus.

VIR (MAN)

The next sign is *Vir*, the man. Closing the hands, thumbs extended, place the base of the hands against the temples, such that the extended thumbs suggest horns. This is the attitude of Pan.

PUELLA (GIRL)

The following sign is *Puella*, or the young girl. This is given by placing the right hand over the left breast and left hand over the genitals, as if to cover up in modesty.

MULIER (WOMAN)

This sign is followed by *Mulier*, or the woman, given by spreading the legs just over shoulder-width and extending the arms above the head and outward, each at a 45-degree angle from the shoulder with the hands open and inward.

MATER TRIUMPHANS (TRIUMPHANT MOTHER)

The final sign is *Mater Triumphans*, or the triumphant mother. It is given by curving the left hand under the solar plexus, as if to cradle a newborn, and the right hand held to the left breast, thumb and index finger touching as if to nurse. The head is bowed, the feet together.

FURTHER READING

Magick (especially Part Three, *Magick in Theory and Practice*)

The Golden Dawn by Israel Regardie

Liber Resh vel Helios

For Crowley, identification with the Sun as a source of life and vitality was extremely important in reclaiming one's own individuality and sense of potency. The sun represents the conscious mind, and therefore the *seat of consciousness and self-awareness*, which is by necessity the center of any individual's world and scope of experience. It is therefore, in a sense, Hadit: the central point of any individual's conscious experience of Nuit. As such, he devised *Liber Resh vel Helios* as a means of attuning the individual with the course and influence of the sun. *Resh* is the Hebrew letter corresponding to the Sun card in the tarot, and *Helios* is the Greek word for the sun itself. This practice is extremely common among Thelemites, who find it extremely empowering, and refer to it as simply "doing Resh."

The purpose of performing Resh is stated in the text of the ritual itself: "Thus shalt thou ever be mindful of the Great Work which thou hast undertaken to perform, and thus shalt thou be strengthened to pursue it to the attainment of the Stone of the Wise, the Summum Bonum, True Wisdom, and Perfect Happiness."[121] Crowley also notes that the

---

121   Crowley, *Magick*, 646.

performance of this ritual will attune the individual to the idea of the sun's apparent "rebirth" at dawn, and that its apparent death is both illusionary and representative of a normal course of events—much like the life of the individual performing it.

Resh consists of four solar adorations at sunrise, midday, sunset, and midnight, and each of these is associated with a particular Egyptian deity that relates to that phase of the sun in its apparent course across the heavens: Ra, Ahathoor, Tum, and Keph-Ra. These four elemental god forms or postures, given previously, accompany each recitation, so you can add these when you feel comfortable with the recitation of the lines.

On a practical note, this ritual instructs you to perform it both at sunrise and at midnight, which may be taken more liberally to mean "upon waking" and "upon going to bed." It is not the purpose of this observation to engage in prolonged sleep deprivation. These should be relatively easy to incorporate into your daily life, with minimal inconvenience, and it will hardly attune your mind to the life-giving, energizing source of our sun if you've not managed more than a few hours' continuous sleep for several weeks!

At Sunrise (Ra)

Greet the sun at dawn, facing east, giving the sign of Shu (air). Say in a loud voice:

Hail unto Thee who art Ra in Thy rising, even unto Thee who art Ra in Thy strength, who travellest over the Heavens in Thy bark at the Uprising of the Sun.

Tahuti standeth in His splendour at the prow, and Ra-Hoor abideth at the helm.

Hail unto Thee from the Abodes of Night!

Give the sign of Silence.

At Midday (Ahathoor)

Greet the sun at noon, facing south, giving the sign of Thoum-aesh-neith (fire). Say in a loud voice:

Hail unto Thee who art Ahathoor in Thy triumphing, even unto Thee who art Ahathoor in Thy beauty, who travellest over the Heavens in Thy bark at the Mid-course of the Sun.

Tahuti standeth in His splendor at the prow, and Ra-Hoor abideth at the helm.

Hail unto thee from the Abodes of Morning!

Give the sign of Silence.

At Sunset (Tum)

Greet the sun at sunset, facing west, giving the sign of Aura-moth (water). Say in a loud voice:

Hail unto Thee who art Tum in Thy setting, even unto Thee who art Tum in Thy joy, who travellest over the Heavens in Thy bark at the Down-going of the Sun.

Tahuti standeth in His splendour at the prow, and Ra-Hoor abideth at the helm.

Hail unto Thee from the Abodes of Day!

Give the sign of Silence.

At Midnight (Khephra)

Greet the sun at midnight, facing north, giving the sign of Set (earth). Say in a loud voice:

Hail unto Thee who art Khephra in Thy hiding, even unto Thee who art Khephra in Thy silence, who travellest over the Heavens in Thy bark at the Midnight Hour of the Sun.

Tahuti standeth in His splendour at the prow, and Ra-Hoor abideth at the helm.

Hail unto Thee from the Abodes of Evening!

Give the sign of Silence.

The cycle of adorations begins anew with the next rising of the sun

The Star Ruby

The Star Ruby was originally published in *The Book of Lies* and later refined in *Magick in Theory and Practice*, part three of the four-part *Magick* (also known as *Liber ABA* or *Book 4*). It represents what Crowley understood as an improvement on the Lesser Banishing Ritual of the Pentagram created by the Golden Dawn. The rite remains elemental in form, substituting new names for each of the quarters based on the Thelemic pantheon. The speaking parts are in Greek, but there is no reason English cannot be used when learning the ritual.

The practice of the Star Ruby includes a preliminary banishment and invocation in the form of the Qabalistic Cross, a modified version from the one that Crowley would have learned from the Golden Dawn, who originated the practice and instead used the Hebrew for the phrase "Thou art the Kingdom, Power, and Mercy forever, Amen." The ritual then proceeds counterclockwise, as this is the traditional direction for banishing—against the direction of the sun, rather than with it when invoking. This ritual can be used as a preliminary to other magical work to clear the temple space, as a general banishing, or simply as an every-day practice for the starting magician.

The Qabalistic Cross

Facing east, in the center, draw deep deep deep thy breath, closing thy mouth with thy right forefinger prest against thy lower lip [sign of Silence]. Then dashing down the hand with a great sweep back and out, expelling forcibly thy breath, cry:

APO PANTOS KAKODAIMONOS! ["Away, every evil spirit!"]

With the same forefinger touch thy forehead, and say SOI, thy member [groin], and say O PHALLE, thy right shoulder, and say ISCHUROS, thy left shoulder, and say EUCHARISTOS; then clasp thine hands, locking the fingers, and cry IAO.

[The Greek means "Thy, O Phallus, Mighty, Beneficient, IAO." *O Phalle* here is intended to mean the generative function, whether male or female.]

Formulation of the Pentagrams

Advance to the East. Imagine strongly a pentagram, aright, in thy forehead. Drawing the hands to the eyes, fling it forth, making the sign of Horus [Sign of the Enterer], and roar THERION! Retire thine hand in the sign of Hoor-paar-Kraat [Sign of Silence].

Go round to the North and repeat; but say NUIT.

Go round to the West and repeat; but whisper BABALON.

Go round to the South and repeat: but bellow HADIT.

Completing the circle widdershins [counterclockwise], retire to the center, and raise thy voice in the Paean, [122] with these words IO PAN, with the signs of N.O.X.

[IO PAN is simply "Hail Pan," as the omnipresent deity.]

Extend the arms in the form of a Tau and say low but clear: PRO MOU IUNGES, OPISO MOU TELETARCHAI, EPI DEXIA MOU SUNOCHEIS, EPARISTERA DAIMONES. PHLEGEI GAR PERI MOU 'O ASTER TON PENTE. KAI EN TEI STELEI 'O ASTER TON 'EX ESTEKE.

---

122 A Paean is a triumphant song or oration: the words "IO PAN" are to be spoken triumphantly.

[Before me the Iynges, behind me, the Teletarchs, to my right the Synoches, to my left the Daimones, for about me flames the pentagram, and in the column stands the hexagram.]

Repeat the Qabalistic Cross, as above, and end as thou didst begin.

Liber V vel Reguli

"Being the Ritual of the Mark of the Beast; an incantation proper to invoke the Energies of the Aeon of Horus, adapted for the daily use of the Magician ... "

—*Liber V vel Reguli*

Liber V vel Reguli is the first ritual we encounter here that is of a very different nature than most magical students and practitioners are accustomed to. To this point, the rituals and customs are reasonably familiar to even the casual student of ceremonial magick, if not modified to suit the energies particular to the Aeon of Horus. For this reason, Reguli often challenges people that are new to Thelema, pushing them out of their comfort zone, while for others it draws them in with something new and exciting—if not taboo!

In the scope of the ritual, one first establishes his or her "Magical East," which is to say their magical orientation, to Boleskine, Crowley's former home on the shores of Loch Ness in northern Scotland. In so doing, the aspirant aligns him—or herself with the magical current of Thelema in a manner similar to that of praying toward Mecca in the Islamic faith. Next, they activate the various *chakras* (energy centers of the body as defined in the practice of yoga) with names from the Thelemic pantheon, vertically with Nuit, Hadit, and Ra-Hoor-Khuit, then horizontally with Aiwaz, Therion, and Babalon. This formulates the Sigil of the Great Hierophant, dependent from the circle, which is Nuit, where the set of vertical and horizontal lines mimics the staff of the Hierophant from the tarot. In full, this serves as a more elaborate version of the Qabalistic Cross seen in the Star Ruby.

Secondly, the magician calls forth the "words of power," or magical formula that defines the method of working within the Aeon of Horus, completing the act with a battery of knocks: 3-5-3, or three knocks and then five, and then three. This indicates the pentagram (five) within the hexagram (three and three), or the indwelling of the macrocosm (god) in the microcosm (individual). Compare this with the introductory battery of knocks, being 1-3-3-3-1, which is more indicative of the sephiroth of the Tree of Life. [123] The word *Abrahadabra* represents a formula indicating the completion of the Great Work, echoing that same idea.

Next, the magician begins to move about to each of the quarters, as is common to many rituals of this sort, with a similar invocation of divine names followed by the signs of N.O.X. However, what is different is the description of the pentagrams; not upright, but averse. For people who have been taught that inverted pentagrams are "evil" and should never be used, this can be quite jarring. However, above and beyond philosophical discussions on what the subjective idea of "evil" really is, there is a good reason for this inversion. After invoking all of the quarters and giving the appropriate signs therein, the magician returns, spiraling, to the center and dropping *downward*, followed by the sign of *Mater Triumphans*—the triumphant mother—the mother having given birth.

That's right: this is a birth ritual.

Aside from a passion play on the birth of the aeon, the birth of Horus, and so on, Liber V vel Reguli can be seen as a powerful ritual for invoking the Thelemic current into your own life by a spiritual rebirth. As the child is inverted in the womb, the pentagrams you have created are actually *upright* from the perspective of the child being born! [124]

---

123   This would imply the first knock as Kether, the final as Malkuth, and the remaining triplicities inclusive of the other sephiroth, including the false sephirah of Daath.

124   DuQuette, *The Magick of Aleister Crowley*, 92.

Finally, the magician invokes "the powers" of AL (god), LA (naught), and ShT, a combination of letters that Crowley understood to mean "force and fire," these being appropriate invocations for the aeon of the hawk-headed and fiery Horus!

The ritual closes with an invocation similar to that seen in the Star Ruby, and a repetition of the opening gesture.

The First Gesture

The Oath of the Enchantment, which is called the Elevenfold Seal.

THE ANIMADVERSION TOWARDS THE AEON [125]

1. Let the Magician, robed and armed as he may deem to be fit, turn his face towards Boleskine, that is the house of the Beast 666.

2. Let him strike the battery 1-3-3-3-1.

3. Let him put the thumb of his right hand between its index and medius, and make the gestures hereafter following.

THE VERTICAL COMPONENT OF THE ENCHANTMENT

1. Let him describe a circle about his head, crying, "NUIT!"

2. Let him draw the thumb vertically downward, and touch the *muladhara chakra* [genitals], crying, "HADIT!"

3. Let him, retracing the line, touch the centre of his breast, and cry, "RA-HOOR-KHUIT!"

THE HORIZONTAL COMPONENTS OF THE ENCHANTMENT

1. Let him touch the Center of his Forehead, his mouth and his larynx, crying, "AIWAZ!"

2. Let him draw his thumb from right to left across his face at the level of the nostrils.

---

125   Animadversion means "moving against," as a criticism. However, in this case, Crowley is combining *anima* or the "inward-looking aspect of the psyche," and *adversion*, which is a "turning toward."

3. Let him touch the Center of his Breast, and his Solar Plexus, crying, "THERION!" [126]

4. Let him draw his Thumb from left to right across his breast, at the level of the sternum.

5. Let him touch the *svadhisthana* [navel] and the *muladhara* [base of the torso] *chakra*, crying, "BABALON!" [127]

6. Let him draw his thumb from right to left across his abdomen, and the level of the hips.

(Thus shall he formulate the Sigil of the Grand Hierophant, but dependent from the Circle.)

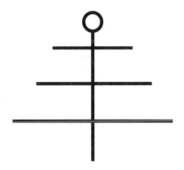

The Sigil of the Grand Hierophant

THE ASSEVERATION OF THE SPELLS [128]

1. Let the Magician clasp his hands upon his wand, his fingers and thumbs interlaced, crying, "LASHTAL! Thelema! FIAOF! AGAPE! AUMGN!"

(Thus shall be declared the Words of Power whereby the Energies of the Aeon of Horus work his Will in the world.)

---

126   Greek for "beast." Crowley also referred to himself as TO MEGA THERION: The Great Beast.

127   The Whore of Babalon; in Thelemic culture, referred to as the complement to the beast (Therion).

128   Asseveration is a strong declaration.

THE PROCLAMATION OF THE ACCOMPLISHMENT

1. Let the Magician strike the battery: 3-5-3, crying, "ABRAHADABRA."

The Second Gesture
THE ENCHANTMENT

1. Let the Magician, still facing Boleskine, advance to the circumference of his Circle.

2. Let him turn himself toward the left, and pace with the stealth and swiftness of a tiger the precincts of his circle, until he complete one revolution thereof.

3. Let him give the Sign of Horus (or the Enterer) as he passeth, so to project the Force that radiateth from Boleskine before him.

4. Let him pace his path until his comes to the north; there let him halt, and turn his face to the North.

5. Let him trace with his wand the Averse Pentagram proper to invoke air (Aquarius). [Starting at the lower left point of the inverted pentagram, draw with the index finger of the right hand a line horizontally to the lower right, then up and across to the upper left, down to the lowermost point, up to the upper right, then down and across to the starting point.]

Averse air

6. Let him bring the Wand to the Centre of the Pentagram and call upon NUIT!

7. Let him make the sign called Puella, standing with his feet together, head slightly bowed to the left, his left hand shielding the muladhara chakra, and his right hand shielding his breast (attitude of the Venus de Medici).

8. Let him turn again to the left, and pursue his path as before, projecting the Force from Boleskine as he passeth; let him halt when he next cometh to the south, and face outward.

9. Let him trace the Averse Pentagram that invoketh fire (Leo). [Starting at the lowermost point, draw a line to the upper left point, then down and across to the lower right, horizontal to the lower left, up and across to the upper right, then back to the point at which you began.]

Averse fire

10. Let him point his Wand to the Centre of the Pentagram, and cry, "HADIT!"

11. Let him give the sign Puer, standing with feet together, and
     head erect. Let his right hand (the thumb extended at right
     angles to the fingers) be raised, the forearm vertical at a right
     angle with the upper arm, which is horizontally extended in the
     line joining the shoulders. Let his left hand, the thumb extend-
     ed forwards, and the fingers clenched, rest at the junction of the
     thighs (attitude of the gods Mentu, Khem, etc.).

12. Let him proceed as before; then in the east, let him make the
     Averse Pentagram that invoketh earth (Taurus). [Starting at the
     lowermost point, draw the line to the upper right, then down
     and across to the lower left, horizontal to the lower right, up and
     across to the upper left, and down again to where you began.]

Averse earth

13. Let him point his wand to the Centre of the Pentagram, and cry,
     "THERION!"

14. Let him give the sign called Vir, the feet being together. The
     hands, with clenched fingers and thumbs thrust out forwards,
     are held to the temples; the head is then bowed and pushed for-
     ward, as if to symbolize the butting of an horned beast (attitude
     of Pan, Bacchus, etc.).

15. Proceeding as before, let him make in the west the Averse Pentagram whereby water is invoked (Scorpio). [Starting at the lower right point, draw the line horizontally across to the lower left, then up and across to the upper right, then down to the lowermost point, up to the upper left, and finally down and to the right to finish.]

Averse water

16. Pointing the wand to the Centre of the Pentagram, let him call upon BABALON!

17. Let him give the sign Mulier. The feet are widely separated, and the arms raised so as to suggest a crescent. The head is thrown back (attitude of Baphomet, Isis in Welcome, the Microcosm of Vitruvius).

18. Let him break into the dance, tracing a centripetal spiral widdershins [counterclockwise], enriched by revolutions upon his axis as he passeth each Quarter, until he come to the Centre of the Circle. There let him halt, facing Boleskine.

19. Let him raise the Wand, trace the Mark of the Beast [below], and cry, "AIWAZ!" [129]

The Mark of the Beast

20. Let him trace the Invoking Hexagram of the Beast. [Starting at the uppermost point, draw down to the lower right, across to the upper left, down to the lowermost, up to the upper right, across to the lower left, then returning to the topmost point.]

The Invoking Hexagram of the Beast

---

129   (The most simple form of the Mark of the Beast is the conjoined form of the sun and moon at the head of this elaborate figure.)

21. Let him lower the wand, striking the earth therewith.

22. Let him give the sign of Mater Triumphans. (The feet are together; the left arm is curved as if it supported a child, the thumb and index finger of the right hand pinch the nipple of the left breast, as if offering it to that child.) Let him utter the word, "THELEMA!"

23. Perform the Spiral Dance, moving deosil and whirling widdershins. Each time on passing the West extend the Wand to the Quarter in question and bow:

    a. Before me the Powers of LA! (to West)

    b. Behind me the Powers of AL! (the East)

    c. On my right hand the Powers of LA! (to North)

    d. On my left hand the Powers of AL! (to South)

    e. Above me the Powers of ShT! (leaping in the air)

    f. Below me the Powers of ShT! (striking the ground)

    g. Within me the powers! (in the attitude of Ptah, erect, the feet together, the hands clasped upon the vertical Wand.)

    h. About me flames my Father's Face, the Star of Force and Fire!

    i. And in the Column stands His six-rayed Splendour!

(This dance may be omitted, and the whole utterance chanted in the attitude of Ptah.) [130]

The Final Gesture
This is identical with the First Gesture.

---

130   In Egyptian mythology, Ptah is depicted as holding a staff or wand upright with both hands.

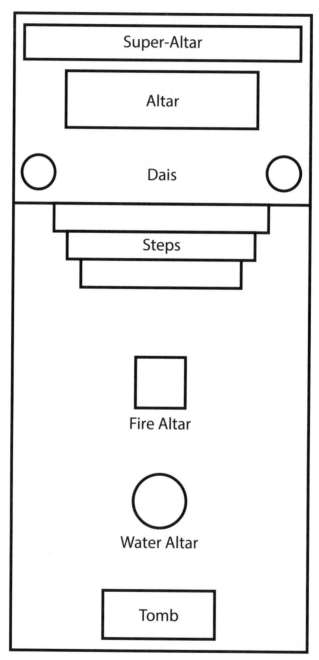

The layout for the temple of the Gnostic Mass

The Gnostic Mass

One of the simplest and most complete of Magick ceremonies is the Eucharist. It consists of taking common things, transmuting them into things divine, and consuming them.

—Crowley, *Magick*, Part Three, Chapter XX.

Crowley notes that the Gnostic Mass is the "central public and private ritual of the O.T.O.," created in a flurry of inspiration while traveling in Russia in 1913, writing it "under the influence of the Liturgy of St. Basil of the Russian Church." It was first published in a periodical called *The International* in 1918, and later in 1919 in Crowley's own publication, *The Equinox, Vol. III, No. I.* He also included it in an appendix to *Magick in Theory and Practice* in 1929/30. It is worth noting that while I can describe the Gnostic Mass herein and provide some personal thoughts on its practice and meaning, final authority rests with the Ecclesia Gnostica Catholica, and I defer any definitive position to that organization. The Gnostic Mass is a complex and lengthy ritual in comparison to those given previously, performed by a priest, a priestess, a deacon, and two children, and shared by the congregants, who are active participants themselves. Thus, I do not include it here as something I expect you to do at home, but rather as something you could *experience* at a local body of the O.T.O., should that be your desire. As a whole, the ritual can be interpreted as a passion play between an individual (the priest) and the universe (the priestess), united by love in ecstatic union, wherein the deacon serves as the intermediary between the two, much as the HGA might in one's personal experience. The children are present as countercharged, positive/active and negative/passive forces that attend the elemental weapons on the altars of fire (and air) and water (and earth), respectively.

The priest's journey begins, as it does with so many aspirants, in a tomb in the west. He is spiritually unawakened until the priestess emerges, descends unto him, and calls him forth with a consecration that allows him to realize his true purpose. He then elevates and enshrines the priestess upon the altar. When they finally reunite, it allows for the "miracle of the mass,"[131] wherein the Eucharist becomes the vehicle of the will of the priest, thereby each and every congregant in turn.

The layout of the temple for the Gnostic Mass is worth reviewing, and is reminiscent of the Tree of Life as a symbolic representation of the cosmos. The Tomb, as mentioned, is set in the west of the temple, the place of the dying sun in Egyptian mythology. Opposite this is an elaborate altar set on a dais, or raised platform, preceded by three steps. This altar is where the priestess remains once she is enthroned by the priest in (and through) adoration, having a bouquet of roses on each side, as well as two large candles. Above this altar is a super-altar of two tiers: the first holds *The Book of the Law* flanked by six candles on each side, while the second and uppermost holds an image of the Stele of Revealing flanked by four candles on each side. Two large pillars flank the front edge of the dais, in offset black and white, and the entirety of the dais is concealed within a large veil. The steps remain outside of the veil, however, as the Priest ascends them in approaching the altar. Between the tomb and dais are two smaller altars, one being the fire altar, containing the active elements of fire and air, and the other being the water altar, referred to as the *font* and containing the elements of water and earth. The priestess and the priest use these elements to consecrate each other in the opening of the Gnostic Mass, with the aid of the children. The deacon is generally situated at the base of the fire altar unless attending to other duties within the performance of the ritual.

With the priest always being male and the priestess always being female, the performance of the Gnostic Mass has led to some discussion in Thelemic culture about gender roles and liturgical assignment—enough so that it bears comment here. Even with more traditional religious institutions opening the doors to women in the priesthood, it seems oddly archaic that such a reportedly progressive philosophy should assert the necessity of

---

131   Given in the Creed of the Gnostic Mass, hereafter.

gender assignment in these roles. [132] (I will note that the roles of priest and priestess are considered coequal, rather than hierarchical in one direction or another, as in many other religions.) The reason for this gender specificity is a simple one, in that Crowley was writing the Gnostic Mass with a *specific magical formula in mind* with a masculine principle, and as such was the only one that he could write as a man himself. It's not that a similar feminine formula does not or could not exist, but Crowley would have been singularly unqualified to write it because he lacked the right equipment! Personally, I don't believe that Crowley could or should have written a complementary mass from a feminine perspective for the simple fact that he would have been operating out of conjecture. He simply did not have the psyche of a female to comprehend the true nature of the mass from that vantage.

Personally, I find the Gnostic Mass to be an exceptionally beautiful ritual to perform or simply experience as a congregant. While the clergy administer the rite as described, the congregants are actively involved in the performance, with explicit actions and orations throughout, starting with the recitation of the Creed. There will typically be a review of these actions prior to a celebration of the mass that describes the actions specific to the congregation, each at the direction of the deacon, whose job it is—in part—to marshal the congregants as necessary.

Dieu Garde

This is the default position when standing. The feet are "square," meaning the left foot facing forward and the right at a ninety-degree angle with the heel against the instep of the left. The hands are held flat in front, loosely, with the thumbs linked.

---

132   As of this writing, the EGC asserts the gender assignment of Priest and Priestess as male and female, respectively, but does allow for transgender persons to take the role with which they identify.

Step and Sign of a Man and a Brother

This action is performed by the deacon and congregants prior to the recitation of the Creed. The step is given by starting at Dieu Garde, advancing the left foot and then drawing the right back to square. This is followed by placing the thumb of the right hand at the level of the throat, fingers extended and palm parallel to the floor, drawing it sharply across the throat from left to right. Return to Dieu Garde.

Hailing Sign of a Magician

Place the right hand sideways over the heart, the thumb extended at a right angle to the fingers so that it points upward. The left hand is held open (extending the thumb in the same manner) with the upper arm straight out from the body and forearm upward at a right angle to the upper arm. This sign is given several times in the early stages of the mass, following the deacon.

Flame of Adoration

As the priest begins his ascent to the high altar, the deacon, children, and congregants kneel, the hands held above the head, joined palm to palm.

Attitude of Resurrection

At the conclusion of the mass, all present communicate—that is, partake of the Eucharist, a glass of wine and Cake of Light (communion wafer). The host is made according to the recipe given in *The Book of the Law*, chapter III, 23–25:

> For perfume, mix meal & honey & thick leavings of red wine [133]: then oil of Abramelin and olive oil, and afterward soften and smooth down with rich, fresh blood.

---

133 Leavings are the remnants of the fermentation process in red wine, where the skins of the grapes are left.

The best blood is of the moon, monthly: then the fresh blood of a child, or dropping from the host of heaven: then of enemies; then of the priest or of the worshippers: last of some beast, no matter what.

This burn: of this make cakes & eat unto me ...

This recipe requires some explanation and reference to common practice. First, "oil of Abramelin" comes from a recipe given in that same work, consisting of olive oil, cinnamon, and a number of similar ingredients. The raw cinnamon gives a warming sensation when applied to the skin, and it is commonly used in Western ceremonial magick. Given that Ra-Hoor-Khuit, in whose voice the third chapter is written, is a god of war, the fact that blood is involved should not come as much of a surprise. Blood is particularly associated with the planet Mars, which rules over concepts of war. The text then goes on to describe the qualities of the blood in respect to how it is gathered, and from what or whom.[134] The biological material is then burned to ash, which satisfies us that any blood-borne contaminants are thus eradicated, and thereafter reintroduced for the purpose of the Gnostic Mass in the recipe given in III:23, the admixture of meal, honey, and leavings.

Following the consumption of the Eucharist, each congregant then echoes the priest's words, "There is no part of me that is not of the gods." The arms are then crossed over the chest in an "attitude of resurrection," right over left, with the tips of the fingers at the shoulders. This is the same as the Sign of Osiris (Risen), given previously.

Striking the Breast

The priest strikes his breast two times during the course of the mass using the closed fist of the right hand against the left breast. On the first of these strikes, the deacon and congregants repeat this action following

---

134   If it has crossed your mind: no, the congregants at a Gnostic Mass are never asked to give their blood to make the host. These are prepared ahead of time, typically using the last of the stated ingredients.

the line "Hear ye all, saints of the true church of old time, now essentially present, that of ye we claim heirship, with ye we claim communion, and from ye we claim benediction in the name IAO."

Many local bodies of Ordo Templi Orientis celebrate the Gnostic Mass regularly, and these celebrations are generally open to the public unless otherwise stated. If you are interested in attending one, contact your nearest O.T.O. body for more information, the details for which are provided hereafter in the final chapter.

It is otherwise given here with minimal commentary.

Of the Furnishings of the Temple [135]

IN THE EAST, that is, in the direction of Boleskine, which is situated on the southeastern shore of Loch Ness in Scotland, two miles east of Foyers, is a shrine, or High Altar. Its dimensions should be seven feet in length, three feet in breadth, and forty-four inches in height. It should be covered with a crimson altar-cloth, on which may be embroidered a fleur-de-lis in gold, or a sunblaze or other suitable emblem.

On each side of it should be a pillar or obelisk with countercharges in black and white.

Below it should be a dais of three steps in black and white squares.

Above it is the super-altar, at whose top is the Stele of Revealing in reproduction, with four candles on each side of it. Below the stele is a place for *The Book of the Law*, with six candles on each side of it. Below this again is the Holy Graal, with roses on each side of it. There is room in front of the Cup for the Paten. On each side beyond the roses are two great candles.

All this is enclosed within a great Veil.

Forming the apex of an equilateral triangle whose base is a line drawn between the pillars is a small, black, square altar of superimposed cubes.

---

135   The text of the Gnostic Mass is taken from Crowley in *Magick*. There are subtle, but generally nonsubstantiative, differences even in the several approved publications.

This altar is the base of a similar and equal triangle, and at the apex of this second triangle is a small circular font.

Repeating, the apex of a third triangle is an upright coffin or tomb.

Of the Officers of the Mass

- **The Priest** bears the Sacred Lance and is clothed at first in a plain white robe.
- **The Priestess** should be actually virgo Intacta or specially dedicated to the service of the Great Order. She is clothed in white, blue, and gold. She bears the sword from a red girdle, and the Paten and Hosts, or Cakes of Light.
- **The Deacon** is clothed in white and yellow. He bears *The Book of the Law*.
- **Two Children** are clothed in white and black. One bears a pitcher of water and a cellar of salt, the other a censer of fire and a casket of perfume.

Of the Ceremony of the Introit [136]

The DEACON, opening the door of the Temple, admits the congregation and takes his stand between the small altar and the font. (There should be a doorkeeper to attend the admission.)

The DEACON advances and bows before the open shrine where the Graal is exalted. He kisses *The Book of the Law* three times, opens it, and places it upon the super-altar. He turns west.

The DEACON: Do what thou wilt shall be the whole of the Law. I proclaim the Law of Light, Life, Love and Liberty, in the name of IAO.

The CONGREGATION: Love is the law, love under will.

---

136   The introit is the entry ceremony of a religious service.

The DEACON goes to his place between the altar of incense and the font, faces east, and gives the step and sign of a Man and a Brother. All imitate him.

The DEACON and all the PEOPLE:

I believe in one secret and ineffable Lord; and one Star in the Company of Stars of whose fire we are created, and to which we shall return; and in one Father of Life, Mystery of Mystery, in His name CHAOS, the sole vice-regent of the Sun upon the Earth; and in one Air, the nourisher of all that breathes.

And I believe in one Earth, the Mother of us all, and in one Womb wherein all men are begotten and wherein they shall rest, Mystery of Mystery, in her name BABALON.

And I believe in the Serpent and the Lion, Mystery of Mystery, in his name BAPHOMET.

And I believe in one Gnostic and Catholic Church of Light, Life, Love and Liberty, the word of whose law is THELEMA.

And I believe in the Communion of Saints.

And, forasmuch as meat and drink are transmuted in us daily into spiritual substance, I believe in the Miracle of the Mass.

And I confess one Baptism of Wisdom whereby we accomplish the Miracle of Incarnation.

And I confess my Life, one, individual, and eternal, that was, and is, and is to come.

AUMGN. AUMGN. AUMGN.

Music is now played. The child enters with the ewer and salt.[137] The VIRGIN enters with the Sword and Paten. The child enters with the censer and perfume. They face the DEACON, deploying into line, from the space between the two altars.

The VIRGIN: Greeting of Earth and Heaven!

All give the Hailing Sign of a Magician, the DEACON leading.

The PRIESTESS, the negative child on her left, the positive child on her right, ascends the steps of the High Altar. They await her below. She places the Paten before the Graal. Having adored it, she descends, and with the children following her, the positive next to her, she moves in a serpentine manner involving three and a half circles of the Temple. (Deosil about the altar, widdershins about the font, deosil about the altar and font, widdershins about the altar, and so to the Tomb in the West.) She draws her Sword and pulls down the Veil therewith.

The PRIESTESS: By the Power of Iron ✠, I say to unto thee
Arise. In the name of our Lord ✠ the Sun, and of our Lord ✠,
that thou mayst administer the virtues to the Brethren.

She sheathes the Sword.

The PRIEST, having issued from the Tomb, holding the lance erect with both hands, right over left, against his breast, takes the first three regular steps. He then gives the Lance to the PRIESTESS and gives the three penal signs.[138]

He kneels and worships the Lance with both hands.
Penitential music.

The PRIEST: I am a man among men.

He takes again the Lance, and lowers it. He rises.

---

137   A ewer is a large-mouthed pitcher.

138   These are given by drawing the hand horizontally across the throat, solar plexus, and hips.

The PRIEST: How should I be worthy to administer the virtues to the Brethren?

The PRIESTESS takes from the child the water and the salt, and mixes them in the font.

The PRIESTESS: Let the salt of Earth admonish the Water to bear the virtue of the Great Sea. (Genuflects) Mother, be thou adored.

She returns to the west. ✠ on PRIEST with open hand doth she make, over his forehead, breast, and body.

Be the PRIEST pure of body and soul!

The PRIESTESS takes the censer [and perfume] from the child, and places it on the small altar. She puts incense therein.

Let the Fire and Air make sweet the world! (Genuflects) Father, be thou adored.

She returns to the West, and makes ✠ with the censer before the PRIEST, thrice, as before.

Be the PRIEST fervent of body and soul!

(The children resume their weapons as they are done with.)

The DEACON now takes the consecrated robe from the High Altar and brings it to her. She robes the PRIEST in his robe of scarlet and gold.

Be the flame of the Sun thine ambiance, O thou PRIEST of the SUN!

The DEACON brings the crown from the High Altar. (The crown may be of gold or platinum, or of electrum magicum; but with no other metals, save the small proportions necessary to a proper alloy. It may be adorned with diverse jewels, at will, but must have the Uraeus Serpent twined about it, and the cap of maintenance must match the scarlet of the Robe. Its texture should be velvet.)

Be the Serpent thy crown, O thou PRIEST of the LORD!

Kneeling, she takes the Lance between her open hands and runs them up and down the shaft eleven times, very gently.

Be the LORD present among us!

All give the Hailing Sign.

The PEOPLE: **So mote it be.**

Of the Ceremony of the Opening of the Veil

The PRIEST: Thee therefore whom we adore, we also invoke.
By the power of the lifted Lance!

He raises the Lance. All repeat Hailing Sign.
A phrase of triumphant music.
The PRIEST take the PRIESTESS by her right hand with his left, keeping the Lance raised.

I, PRIEST and KING, take thee VIRGIN pure without spot; I upraise thee; I lead thee to the East; I set thee upon the summit of the Earth.

He thrones the PRIESTESS upon the altar. The DEACON and the children follow, they in rank, behind him. The PRIESTESS takes *The Book of the Law*, resumes her seat, and holds it open on her breast with her two hands, making a descending triangle with thumbs and forefingers.

The PRIEST gives the Lance to the DEACON to hold, and takes the ewer from the child, and sprinkles the PRIESTESS, making five crosses, forehead, shoulders, and thighs.

The thumb of the PRIEST is always between his index and medius, whenever he is not holding the Lance. The PRIEST takes the censer from the child, and makes five crosses as before. The children replace their weapons[139] on their respective altars.

---

139   The ewer and censer.

The PRIEST kisses *The Book of the Law* three times. He kneels for a space in adoration, with joined hands, knuckles closed, thumb in position aforesaid.

He rises, and draws the veil over the whole altar.

All rise and stand to order.

The PRIEST takes the Lance from the DEACON, and holds it as before, as Osiris or Ptah. He circumambulates the Temple three times, followed by the DEACON and the children as before. (These, when not using their hands, keep their arms crossed upon their breasts.) At the last circumambulation, they leave him, and go to the space between the font and small altar, where they kneel in adoration, their hands joined palm to palm and raised above their heads.

All imitate this motion.

The PRIEST returns to the East, and mounts the first step of the altar.

The PRIEST: O Circle of Stars, whereof our Father is but the younger brother, marvel beyond imagination, soul of infinite space, before whom time is ashamed, the mind bewildered, and the understanding dark, not unto Thee may we attain unless Thine image be Love. Therefore, by seed and root and stem and bud and leaf and flower and fruit do we invoke Thee.

Then the priest answered & said unto the Queen of Space, kissing her lovely brows, the dew of her light bathing his whole body in a sweet-smelling perfume of sweat; O Nuit, continuous one of Heaven, let it be ever thus; that men speak not of thee as One but as None; and let them speak not of thee at all, since Thou art continuous!

During this speech, the PRIESTESS must have divested herself completely of her robe.

The PRIESTESS: But to love me is better than all things; if under my night-stars in the desert thou presently burnest mine incense before me, invoking me with a pure heart, and the serpent flame therein, thou shalt come a little to lie in my bosom. For one kiss wilt thou be willing to give all; but whoso gives one particle of dust shall lose all in that hour. Ye shall gather goods and store of women and spices; ye shall wear rich jewels; ye shall exceed the nations of the earth in splendour and pride; but always in the love of me, and so shall ye come to my joy. I charge you earnestly to come before me in a single robe, and covered with a rich head-dress. I love you! I yearn to you! Pale or purple, veiled or voluptuous, I who am all pleasure and drunkenness of the innermost sense desire you. Put on the wings, and arouse the coiled splendour within you: come to me! To me! To me! Sing the rapturous love-song unto me! Burn to me perfumes! Wear to me jewels! Drink to me, for I love you! I love you. I am the blue-lidded daughter of sunset; I am the naked brilliance of the voluptuous night-sky. To me! To me!

The PRIEST mounts the second step.

The PRIEST: O secret of secrets that art hidden in the being of all that lives, not Thee do we adore, for that which adoreth is also Thou. Thou are That, and That am I.

I am the flame that burns in every heart of man, and in the core of every star. I am Life, and the giver of Life; yet therefore is the knowledge of me the knowledge of Death. I am alone. There is no God where I am.

The DEACON and all present rise to their feet with the Hailing Sign.

The DEACON: But ye, O my people, rise up and awake!

Let the rituals be rightly performed with joy and beauty!

There are rituals of the elements and feasts of the times.

A feast for the First Night of the Prophet and his Bride!

A feast for the three days of the writing of the Book of the Law.

A feast for Tahuti and the child of the Prophet—secret,
O Prophet!

A feast for the Supreme Ritual and a feast for the Equinox of
the Gods.

A feast for fire and a feast for water; a feast for life and a
greater feast for death!

A feast every day in your hearts in the joy of my rapture!

A feast every night unto Nu, and the pleasure of uttermost
delight.

The PRIEST mounts the third step.

The PRIEST: Thou that art one, our Lord in the Universe, the
Sun, our Lord in ourselves whose name is Mystery of Mystery,
uttermost being whose radiance, elightening the worlds, is also
the breath that maketh every God even and Death to tremble
before Thee—By the Sign of Light ✠ appear Thou glorious
upon the throne of the Sun. Make open the path of creation
and of intelligence between us and our minds. Enlighten our
understanding. Encourage our hearts. Let thy light crystalize
itself within our blood, fulfilling us of Resurrection.
A ka dua
Tuf ur biu
Bi a'a chefu
Dudu nur af an nuteru! [140]

---

140   A transliteration of the Stele of Revealing that Crowley adapted poetically as
"Unity uttermost showed! I adore the might of Thy breath, Supreme and terrible God, Who makest the gods and death to tremble before thee—I, I adore
thee!"

The PRIESTESS: There is no law beyond Do what thou wilt.

The PRIEST parts the veil with his lance. During the previous speeches the PRIESTESS has, if necessary, as in savage countries, resumed her robe.

The PRIEST: IO, IO, IO! IAO! SABAO! KURIE ABRASAX, KURIE MITHRAS, KURIE PHALLE! IO PAN! IO PAN! PAN! IO ISCHUROS, IO ATHANATOS, IO ABRATOS, IO IAO! KAIRE PHALLE, KAIRE PANPHAGE, KAIRE PANGE-NETOR! HAGIOS, HAGIOS, HAGIOS, IAO!

The PRIESTESS is seated with the Paten in her right hand and the cup in her left.

The PRIEST presents the Lance, which she kisses eleven times.

She then holds it to her breast, while the PRIEST, falling at her knees, kisses them, his arms stretched along her thighs. He remains in this ado-ration while the DEACON intones the Collects.

All stand to order, with the Dieu Garde, that is, feet square, hands, with the thumbs linked, held loosely. This is the universal position while standing, unless other direction is given.

Of the Office of the Collects Which are Eleven in Number
THE SUN

The DEACON: Lord visible and sensible of whom this earth is but a frozen spark turning about thee with annual and diurnal motion, source of light, source of life, let thy perpetual radi-ance hearten us to continual labour and enjoyment; so that as we are constant partakers in thy bounty we may in our particu-lar orbit give out light and life, sustenance and joy, to them that revolve about us without diminution of substance or effulgence forever.

The PEOPLE: So mote it be.

THE LORD

The DEACON: Lord secret and most holy, source of light, source of life, source of love, source of liberty, be thou ever constant and mighty within us, force of energy, fire of motion; with diligence let us ever labour with thee that we may remain in thine abundant joy.

The PEOPLE: So mote it be.

THE MOON

The DEACON: Lady of night, that turning ever about us art now visible and now invisible in thy season, be thou favorable unto hunters, and lovers, and to all men that toil upon the earth, and all mariners upon the sea.

The PEOPLE: So mote it be.

THE LADY

The DEACON: Giver and receiver of joy, gate of life and love, be thou ever ready, thou and thine handmaiden, in thine office of gladness.

The PEOPLE: So mote it be.

THE SAINTS

The DEACON: Lord of Life and Joy, that art the might of man, that art the essence of every true god that is upon the surface of the earth, continuing knowledge from generation unto generation, thou adored of us upon heaths as in woods, on mountains as in caves, openly in the marketplaces and secretly in the chambers of our houses, in temples of gold and ivory and marble as in these other temples of our bodies, we worthily commemorate them worthy that did of old adore thee and manifest thy glory unto men:

(At each name the DEACON signs with thumb between the index and medius. At ordinary mass it is only necessary to commemorate those whose names are italicized, with wording as shown.)

Lao Tzu and Siddhartha and Krishna and Tahuti, Mosheh, Dionysus, Mohammed, and To Mega Therion, with these also, Hermes, Pan, Priapus, Osiris, and Malchizidek, Khem, and Amoun and Mentu, Heracles, Orpheus and Odysseus; with Vergillus, Catullus, Martialis, Rabelais, Swinburne, and many an holy bard; Appollonius Tyanaeus, Simon Magus, Manes, Pythagoras, Basilides, Valentinus, Bardesanes, and Hippolytus, who transmitted the light of the gnosis to us, their successors and their heirs; with Merlin, Arthur, Kamuret, Parzival, and many another prophet, priest, and king that bore the Lance and Cup, the Sword and Disk, against the Heathen; and these also, Carolus Magnus, and his paladins, with William of Schyren, Frederick of Hohenstaufen, Roger Bacon, Jacobus Burgundus Molensis the Martyr, Christian Rozenkreuz, Ulrich von Hutten, Paracelsus, Michael Maier, Roderic Borgia Pope Alexander the Sixth, Jakob Böhme, Francis Bacon Lord Verulam, Andrea, Robertus de Fluctibus, Giordano Bruno, Johannes Dee, Sir Edward Kelly, Thomas Vaughn, Elias Ashmole, Molinos, Adam Weishaupt, Wolfgang von Goethe, William Blake, Ludovicus Rex Bavariae, Richard Wagner, Alphonse Louis Constant, Friedrich Nietzsche, Hargrave Jennings, Carl Kellner, Forlong dux, Sir Richard Payne Knight, Sir Richard Francis Burton, Paul Gauguin, Doctor Gerard Encausse, Doctor Theodor Reuss, and Sir Aleister Crowley [141]—Oh Sons of the Lion and the Snake! With all thy saints we worthily commemorate them worthy that were and are

---

141   The names of Karl Johannes Germer and Major Grady Louis McMurtry are often included after the name of Aleister Crowley as his (now deceased) successors as head of O.T.O.

and are to come. May their Essence be here present, potent, puissant, and paternal to perfect this feast!

The PEOPLE: So mote it be.

THE EARTH

The DEACON: Mother of fertility on whose breast lieth water, whose cheek is caressed by air, and in whose heart is the sun's fire, womb of all life, recurring grace of seasons, answer favorably the prayer of labor, and to pastors and husbandmen be thou propitious.

The PEOPLE: So mote it be.

THE PRINCIPLES

The DEACON: Mysterious Energy, triform, mysterious matter, in fourfold and sevenfold division, the interplay of which things weave the dance of the Veil of Life upon the Face of the Spirit, let there be Harmony and Beauty in your mystic loves, that in us may be health and wealth and strength and divine pleasure according to the Law of Liberty; let each pursue his Will as a strong man that rejoiceth in his way, as the course of a Star that blazeth forever among the joyous company of Heaven.

The PEOPLE: So mote it be.

BIRTH

The DEACON: Be the hour auspicious, and the gate of life open in peace and in well-being, so that she that beareth children may rejoice, and the babe catch life with both hands.

The PEOPLE: So mote it be.

MARRIAGE

The DEACON: Upon all that this day unite with love under will let fall success; may strength and skill unite to bring forth ecstasy, and beauty answer beauty.

The PEOPLE: So mote it be.

DEATH

All stand, head erect, eyes open.

The DEACON: Term of all that liveth, whose name is inscrutable, be favourable unto us in thine hour.

The PEOPLE: So mote it be.

THE END

The DEACON: Unto them from whose eyes the veil of life hath fallen may there be granted the accomplishment of their true Wills; whether they will absorption in the Infinite, or to be united with their chosen and preferred, or to be in contemplation, or to be at peace, or to achieve the labour and heroism of incarnation on this planet or another, or in any Star, or aught else, unto them may there be granted the accomplishment of their wills; yea, the accomplishment of their wills. AUMGN. AUMGN. AUMGN.

The PEOPLE: So mote it be.

All sit.

The DEACON and the children attend the PREIST and PRIESTESS, ready to hold any appropriate weapon as may be necessary.

Of the Consecration of the Elements

The PRIEST makes the five crosses. 1, 2, 3 on paten and cup; 4 on paten alone; 5 on cup alone. [142]

> The PRIEST: Life of man upon earth, fruit of labour, sustenance of endeavor, thus be thou nourishment of the Spirit!

> The touches the Host with the Lance.

> By the virtue of the Rod!
> Be this bread the Body of God!

> He takes the host.

> **TOUTO ESTI TO SOMA MOU.**
> [This is my body.]

He kneels, adores, rises, turns, shows Host to the PEOPLE, turns, replaces, Host, and adores. Music.

> He takes the Cup.

> Vehicle of the joy of Man upon earth, solace of labour, inspiration of endeavor, thus be thou ecstasy of the Spirit!

> He touches the Cup with the Lance.

> By the virtue of the Rod!
> Be this wine the Blood of God!

> He takes the Cup.

> TOUTO ESTI TO POTERION TOU HAIMATOS MOU.
> [This is the cup of my blood.]

He kneels, adores, rises, turns, shows the Cup to the PEOPLE, turns, replaces the Cup, and adores. Music.

---

142   The first three crosses are in the shape of an equilateral triangle: the first cross being uppermost, second to the lower right, third to the lower left.

For this is the Covenant of Resurrection.

He makes the five crosses on the PRIESTESS.

Accept, O Lord, this sacrifice of life and joy, true warrants of the Covenant of Resurrection.

The PRIEST offers the Lance to the PRIESTESS, who kisses it; he then touches her between the breasts and upon the body. He then flings out his arms upward, as comprehending the whole shrine.

Let this offering be borne upon the waves of Æther to our Lord and Father the Sun that travelleth over the Heavens in his name ON.

He closes his hands, kisses the PRIESTESS between the breasts, and makes three great crosses over the Paten, the Cup, and himself. He strikes his breast. All repeat this action.

Hear ye all, saints of the true church of old time, now essentially present, that of ye we claim heirship, with ye we claim communion, and from ye we claim benediction in the name of IAO.

He makes three crosses on Paten and Cup together. He uncovers the Cup, genuflects, takes the Cup in his left hand and the Host in his right. With the Host he makes the five crosses on the Cup.

He elevates the Host and Cup. The Bell Strikes.

HAGIOS HAGIOS HAGIOS IAO!
[Holy, Holy, Holy IAO.]

He replaces the Host and the Cup and adores.

Of the Office of the Anthem
The PRIEST:
Thou who art I, beyond all I am,
Who hast no nature and no name,
Who art, when all but Thou are gone,

Thou, centre and secret of the Sun,
Thou, hidden spring of all things known
And unknown, Thou aloof, alone,
Thou, the true fire within the reed,
Brooding and breeding, source and seed,
Of life, love, liberty, and light,
Thou beyond speech and beyond sight,
Thee I invoke, my faint fresh fire,
Kindling as mine intents aspire.
Thee I invoke, abiding one,
Thee, centre and secret of the Sun,
And that most holy mystery
Of which the vehicle am I.
Appear, most awful and most mild,
As it is lawful, in thy child!

The CHORUS:
For of the Father and the Son
The Holy Spirit is the norm;
Male-female, quintessential, one,
Man-being veiled in Woman-Form.
Glory and worship in the highest,
Thou Dove, mankid that deifies,
Being that race most royally run
To spring sunshine through winter storm.
Glory and worship be to Thee,
Sap of the world-ash, wonder-tree!

First semi-chorus, MEN:
Glory to Thee from Gilded Tomb!

Second semi-chorus, WOMEN:
Glory to Thee from Waiting Womb!

MEN:

Glory to Thee from earth unploughed!

WOMEN:

Glory to Thee from virgin vowed!

MEN:

Glory to Thee, true Unity
Of the Eternal Trinity!

WOMEN:

Glory to Thee, thou sire and dam
And self of I am that I am!

MEN:

Glory to Thee, beyond all term,
Thy spring of sperm, thy seed and germ!

WOMEN:

Glory to Thee, eternal Sun,
Thou One in Three, Thou Three in One!

CHORUS:

Glory and Worship unto Thee,
Sap of the world-ash, wonder-tree!

(These words are to form the substance of the anthem; but the whole or any part thereof shall be set to music, which may be as elaborate as art can devise. But even should other anthems be authorized by the Father of the Church, this shall hold its place as the first of its kind, the father of all others.)

Of the Mystic Marriage and Consummation of the Elements

The PRIEST takes the Paten between the index and medius of the right hand.

The PRIESTESS clasps the Cup in her right hand.

The PRIEST: Lord most secret, bless this spiritual food unto our bodies, bestowing upon us health and wealth and strength and joy and peace, and that fulfillment of will and of love under will that is perpetual happiness.

He makes ✠ with Paten and kisses it.
He uncovers the Cup, genuflects, rises. Music.
He takes the Host, and breaks it over the Cup.
He replaces the right-hand portion in the Paten.
He breaks off a particle of the left-hand portion.

TOUTO ESTI TO SPERMA MOU. O PATER ESTIN O HUIOS DIA TO PNEUMA HAGION. AUMGN. AUMGN. AUMGN.
[This is my seed. The Father is the Son through the Holy Spirit. AUMGN. AUMGN. AUMGN.]

He replaces the left-hand part of the Host.
The PRIESTESS extends the Lance-point with her left hand to receive the particle.
The PRIEST clasps the Cup in his left hand.
Together, they depress the Lance-point into the Cup.

The PRIEST and the PRIESTESS: HRILIU

The PRIEST takes the Lance.
The PRIESTESS covers the Cup.
The PRIEST genuflects, rises, bows, joins hands. He strikes his breast.

The PRIEST:
O Lion and O Serpent that destroy the destroyer, be mighty among us.

O Lion and O Serpent that destroy the destroyer, be mighty among us.

O Lion and O Serpent that destroy the destroyer, be mighty among us.

The PRIEST joins hands upon the breast of the PRIESTESS, and takes back his Lance.

He turns to the People, lowers and raises the Lance, and makes ✠ upon them.

Do what thou wilt shall be the whole of the Law.

The PEOPLE: Love is the law, love under will.

He lowers the Lance, and turns to East.

The PRIESTESS takes the Lance in her right hand. With her left she offers the Paten.

The PRIEST kneels.

The PRIEST: In my mouth be the essence of the life of the Sun.

He takes the Host with the right hand, makes ✠ with it on the Paten, and consumes it.

Silence.

The PRIESTESS takes, uncovers, and offers the Cup, as before.

The PRIEST: In my mouth be the essence of the joy of the earth!

He takes the Cup, makes ✠ on the PRIESTESS, drains it, and returns it.

Silence.

He rises, takes the Lance, and turns to the PEOPLE.

The PRIEST: There is no part of me that is not of the gods.

Those of the PEOPLE who intend to communicate, and none other should be present, having signified their intention, a whole Cake of Light, and a whole goblet of wine, have been prepared for each one. The DEACON marshals them; they advance one by one to the altar. The children take the Elements and offer them. The PEOPLE communicate as did the

PRIEST, uttering the same words in an attitude of Resurrection: "There is no part of me that is not of the gods." The exceptions to this part of the ceremony are when it is of the nature of a celebration, which case none but the PRIEST communicate; or part of the ceremony of marriage, when none other, save the two to be married, partake; part of the ceremony of baptism, when only the child baptized partakes; and of Confirmation at puberty, when only the persons confirmed partake. The Sacrament may be reserved by the PRIEST for administration to the sick in their homes.

The PRIEST closes all within the veil.

With the Lance he makes ✠ on the people thrice, thus.

The PRIEST:

✠ The LORD bless you.

✠ The LORD enlighten your minds and comfort your hearts and sustain your bodies.

✠ The LORD bring you to the accomplishment of your true Wills, the Great Work, the Summum Bonum, True Wisdom, and Perfect Happiness.

He goes out, the DEACON and children following, into the tomb of the West.

Music. (Voluntary.)

NOTE: The PRIESTESS and other officers never partake of the Sacrament, they being as it were part of the PRIEST himself.

NOTE: Certain secret formulae of this Mass are taught to the PRIEST in his Ordination.

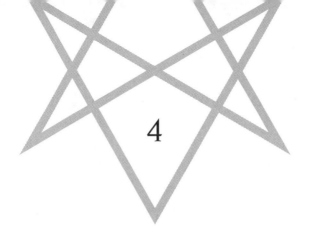

4

Modern Thelema

Thelema is more active and vibrant today than it has ever been, and Crowley's image, life, and work are increasingly more accessible. This is evidenced not only by the increase in popular culture references with each passing year, but also through attention from scholarly and academic research bringing new light to the cultural phenomenon, past and present, that both Crowley and Thelema represent. This new fascination with Crowley's life and work has introduced thousands of new people to Thelema and encouraged thousands more to reevaluate Crowley after decades of association with the now dated devil-worshipping legend of popular culture.

While there are many, *many* people who consider themselves Thelemites and fall under the category of solitary practitioners, Crowley's legacy in the present day primarily continues through the organizations with which he was involved: the O.T.O. and the A∴A∴.

Ordo Templi Orientis (O.T.O.)

One of the most visible legacies of Crowley's magical writings and teaching lives within the first magical order to accept the law of Thelema, the

Ordo Templi Orientis—the Order of Eastern Templars, or Order of the Temple of the East. In form, the O.T.O. is founded on Masonic lines, with degrees that gradually lead the initiate toward the greater understanding of its mysteries.

Following Crowley's death in 1947, the leadership of the O.T.O. was passed to Karl Germer (Frater Saturnus), a lifelong supporter of Crowley who had grown up in Germany and emigrated to the United States after the second world war. Germer died fifteen years later in 1962, unfortunately leaving the Order without a named successor. It was not until 1969 that Grady Louis McMurtry (Hymenaeus Alpha) resurrected the Order based on the authority of letters from Crowley himself. Under McMurtry's leadership, the O.T.O grew out of California's San Francisco Bay area and spread to other major cities across the United States. The current head of the Order, Hymenaeus Beta, is largely responsible for bringing the Order into the prominence that it enjoys today, as well as the large volume of scholarship he has provided and fostered on Crowley's life and works.

Unlike traditional Masonic organizations, the O.T.O. admits both men and women, provided they are free and of full age according to the country in which they reside. The structure of the Order is divided into three distinct strata, based on *The Book of the Law*, "For there are therein Three Grades, the Hermit, the Lover, and the man of Earth." [143] Each initiate begins in the Man of Earth triad, which consists of the following grades: [144]

Degree	Designation	Cycle
0°	Minerval	The Ego is attracted to the Solar System.
I°	Initiation	The Child experiences Birth.
II°	Consecration	The Man or Woman experiences Life.
III°	Devotion	He [She] experiences Death.

143   *Liber AL vel Legis*; I:40.

144   Crowley; *The Equinox, Volume III, No. 10*; 200. Reprinted from *Magick Without Tears*.

Degree	Designation	Cycle
IV°	Perfection (also given as "exaltation")	He [She] experiences the World beyond Death.
P.I.°	Perfect Initiate	This entire cycle of Point-Events is withdrawn into Annihilation.

Crowley notes that all subsequent degrees of the Order are simply elaborations on the Second Degree (Consecration), as this degree represents the life of the individual. "The Rituals V°-IX° are then instructions to the Candidate how he should conduct himself; and they confer upon him, gradually, the Magickal Secrets which make him Master of Life." [145]

The Ecclesia Gnostica Catholica (EGC), or Gnostic Catholic Church, also operates within the scope of the Ordo Templi Orientis, with authority over celebrations of the Gnostic Mass.

As of this writing, the O.T.O. has thousands of members across the globe.

FURTHER READING

The Equinox, Volume III, No. 10

Liber LII—Manifesto of O.T.O.

Liber CI—An Open Letter to Those
Who May Wish to Join the Order

Liber CXCIV—An Intimation with Reference
to the Constitution of the Order

CONTACT INFORMATION

http://www.oto.org

---

145 Crowley, *The Equinox, Volume III, No. 10*, 200.

A∴A∴

Separate from the social organization of the O.T.O., the A∴A∴ (Argentium Astrum, [146] or Silver Star) is specifically a solitary organization dedicated to the spiritual advancement of the individual. Initiates of the A∴A∴ are tested on the grounds of real magical and mystical attainment before being allowed to progress to the next level, and every individual—at least in principle—knows only his or her mentor and those initiates he or she might oversee.

The structure of the A∴ A∴ is also divided into three initiatory strata, which from the lowest to highest are the Order of the Golden Dawn, the Order of the Rosy Cross, and the Order of the Silver Star, as given in Crowley's own prospectus on the Order, *One Star in Sight: A Glimpse of the Structure and System of the Great White Brotherhood* A∴A∴. [147] The Order has eleven grades and depends on real and demonstrable spiritual attainment within each grade to progress, with each grade being associated with a specific sphere on the Qabalistic Tree of Life, just as its predecessor the Golden Dawn had done, and from which it borrows its structure. The corresponding numbers indicate the degree and sephirah (of the Tree of Life), respectively.

The Order of the Silver Star

Ipsissimus .... $10°=1°$
Magus .... $9°=2°$
Magister Templi .... $8°=3°$

---

146   There are other accounts of what A∴ A∴ stands for, including variant spellings, such as Argentum Astrum, *Astron Argon*, and so forth. Crowley notes in *Magick* (p. 479) that the actual meanings of the letters are not disclosed to the profane to thwart "certain swindlers."

147   This can be found most readily in an appendix to *Magick*.

The Order of the Rosy Cross
Babe of the Abyss—the link
Adeptus Exemptus .... 7°=4°
Adeptus Major .... 6°=5°
Adeptus Minor .... 5°=6°

The Order of the Golden Dawn
Dominus Liminus—the link
Philosophus .... 4°=7°
Practicus .... 3°=8°
Zelator .... 2°=9°
Neophyte............... 1°=10°
Probationer .... 0°=0°

There is also the grade of "student," before even "probationer," whose task is to acquire a general knowledge of spiritual systems of attainment.

The A∴A∴ in its current manifestations are independently directed by several separate claimants, with different students of Crowley's having taken up the mantle of his esoteric order. I have listed two initiatory branches herein, with the caveat that there are others that may be more suited or geographically convenient to you.

FURTHER READING
One Star in Sight by Crowley

CONTACT INFORMATION
http://www.outercol.org
http://www.onestarinsight.org

Love is the law, love under will.

—Aleister Crowley

Bibliography

Anonymous. *Hatha Yoga Pradipika*. Translated by Pancham Sinh. New Delhi, India: Munshiram Manoharlal Publishers Pvt Ltd., 1997.

Anonymous. *The Siva Samhita*. Translated by Rai Babdur Srisa Chandra Vasu. New Delhi, India: Munshiram Manoharlal Publishers Pvt Ltd., 1996.

Campbell, Colin. *A Concordance to the Holy Books of Thelema*. York Beach, ME: Teitan Press, 2008.

Churton, Tobias. *Aleister Crowley: The Beast in Berlin: Art, Sex, and Magick in the Weimar Republic*. Rochester, VT: Inner Traditions, 2014.

Churton, Tobias. *Aleister Crowley: The Biography*. London: Watkins Publishing, 2011.

Crowley, Aleister. *Amrita*. Edited by Martin P. Starr. Kings Beach, CA: Thelema Publications, 1990.

———. *The Book of the Law*. York Beach, ME: Samuel Weiser, Inc., 1976.

———. *The Book of Lies*. York Beach, ME: Samuel Weiser, Inc., 1995.

———. *The Book of Thoth*. London: O.T.O., 1944.

———. *Liber Aleph: The Book of Wisdom or Folly*. York Beach, ME: Samuel Weiser, Inc., 2001.

——. *The Commentaries of AL: Being the Equinox*, Vo. 5 No. 1. Edited by Marcelo Ramos Motta. York Beach, ME: Samuel Weiser, Inc., 1975.

——. *The Complete Works, Vol. 1–3*. Foyers, Edinburgh, Scotland: Society for the Propagation of Religious Truth, 1905. Facsimile reprint by Yogi Publication Society, Des Plaines, IL.

——. *The Confessions of Aleister Crowley: An Autohagiography*. Edited by John Symonds and Kenneth Grant. London, Boston, Henley: Routledge & Kegan Paul Ltd., 1979.

——. *The Equinox of the Gods*. London: O.T.O., 1936.

——. *The Equinox, Vol. I, No. 1–10*. York Beach, ME: Samuel Weiser, Inc., 1993.

——. *The Equinox, Vol. III, No. 1*. York Beach, ME: Samuel Weiser, Inc., 1995.

——. *The Equinox, Vol. III, No. 10*. York Beach, ME: Samuel Weiser, Inc., 1990.

——. *The General Principles of Astrology*. With Evangeline Adams. York Beach, ME: Samuel Weiser, Inc., 2002.

——. *The Goetia*. Foyers, Scotland: Society for the Propagation of Religious Truth, 1904.

——. *The Holy Books of Thelema*. York Beach, ME: Samuel Weiser, Inc., 1988.

——. *Little Essays Toward Truth*. Tempe, AZ: New Falcon Publications, 1996.

——. *Magick: Liber ABA: Book 4*. York Beach, ME: Samuel Weiser, Inc., 1994.

——. *Magick Without Tears*. Tempe, AZ: New Falcon Publications, 1991.

——. *777 and Other Qabalistic Writings of Aleister Crowley*. Edited by Israel Regardie. York Beach, ME: Samuel Weiser, Inc., 1996.

Crowley, Aleister [George Archibald Bishop, psued.]. *White Stains*. Privately printed, 1898.

Eckartshausen, Karl von. *The Cloud upon the Sanctuary*. Edited by E. A. Waite. Translated by Isabel de Steiger. London: William Rider & Son, 1909.

Fortune, Dion. *The Mystical Qabalah*. York Beach, ME: Samuel Weiser, Inc., 1993.

Kaczynski, Richard. *Perdurabo: The Life of Aleister Crowley*. Berkeley, CA: North Atlantic Books, 2010. Revised and Expanded Edition.

Kennedy, Maev. "Black Magician Aleister Crowley's Early Gay Verse Comes to Light," *The Guardian*. May 9, 2014.

Mathers, S. L. MacGregor. *The Book of the Sacred Magic of Abramelin the Mage*. New York: Dover Publications, 1975.

——. *The Kabbalah Unveiled*. London: Arkana/Penguin, 1991.

Neatby, William Blair. *A History of the Plymouth Brethren*. London: Hodder and Stoughton, 1901. Archive.org. Accessed November 27, 2015.

Reeve, W. *The New Guide to Leamington Spa, the Neighboring Towns, and Surrounding Country*. London: Privately printed. 1839.

Regardie, Israel. *The Golden Dawn*. St. Paul, MN: Llewellyn Publications, 1993.

Reynolds-Ball, E. A. *Cairo of To-day (Black's Guide Books)*. London: Arnold and Charles Black, 1899.

Spence, Richard. *Secret Agent 666*. Port Townsend, WA: Feral House, 2008.

Sutin, Lawrence. *Do What Thou Wilt: A Life of Aleister Crowley*. New York: St. Martin's Press, 2000.

Vivekananda, Swami. *Raja-Yoga*. New York: Ramakrishna-Vivekananda Center, 1982.

Wilkinson, Louis. *Seven Friends*. London: Mandrake Press, Ltd., 1992.

Worms, Abraham von. *The Book of Abramelin*. Edited by George Dehn. Translated by Stephen Guth. Lake Worth, FL: Ibis Press, 2006.

Index

GET MORE AT LLEWELLYN.COM

Visit us online to browse hundreds of our books and decks, plus sign up to receive our e-newsletters and exclusive online offers.

- Free tarot readings • Spell-a-Day • Moon phases
- Recipes, spells, and tips • Blogs • Encyclopedia
- Author interviews, articles, and upcoming events

GET SOCIAL WITH LLEWELLYN

Find us on   @LlewellynBooks

www.Facebook.com/LlewellynBooks

GET BOOKS AT LLEWELLYN

LLEWELLYN ORDERING INFORMATION

 Order online: Visit our website at www.llewellyn.com to select your books and place an order on our secure server.

 Order by phone:
- Call toll free within the US at 1-877-NEW-WRLD (1-877-639-9753)
- We accept VISA, MasterCard, American Express, and Discover

 Order by mail:
Send the full price of your order (MN residents add 6.875% sales tax) in US funds plus postage and handling to: Llewellyn Worldwide, 2143 Wooddale Drive, Woodbury, MN 55125-2989

POSTAGE AND HANDLING
STANDARD (US):
(Please allow 12 business days)
$30.00 and under, add $6.00.
$30.01 and over, FREE SHIPPING.

INTERNATIONAL ORDERS,
INCLUDING CANADA:
$16.00 for one book, plus $3.00 for each additional book.

Visit us online for more shipping options. Prices subject to change.

FREE CATALOG!

To order, call
1-877-NEW-WRLD
ext. 8236
or visit our website

ALEISTER CROWLEY

— AND —

DION FORTUNE

The Logos of the Aeon and the Shakti of the Age

ALAN RICHARDSON

Aleister Crowley and Dion Fortune
The Logos of the Aeon and the Shakti of the Age
ALAN RICHARDSON

Aleister Crowley and Dion Fortune were two of the most controversial and powerful occultists of the 20th century. Crowley was regarded by many as a creature of the night, albeit one whose soul was streaked with brilliance; Fortune was viewed as one of the Shining Ones, who nevertheless wrestled with her own darkness. Between them they produced some of the best books on magick ever written, and their influence upon contemporary magicians has been profound.

Written by occult scholar Alan Richardson, this unusual and provocative book draws upon unpublished material to reveal little-known aspects of Crowley and Fortune's relationship, and their role as harbingers of sweeping cultural changes—foreshadowing the women's movement, the sexual revolution, and 1960s counterculture—as well as other surprising influences upon our present culture.

978-0-7387-1580-3, 6 x 9, 216 pp. $18.95

To order, call 1-877-NEW-WRLD
Prices subject to change without notice
Order at Llewellyn.com 24 hours a day, 7 days a week!